Captivating craziness of a life woven and chosen by Christ to be a voice of victory for generations and nations! Hope lines these pages of Greg's story that everyone needs to hear!

KATHY BRANZELL, president of the National Day of Prayer Task Force

Greg's memoir deeply reminded me there is no sin too great nor sinner too far gone that Jesus cannot forgive or save. Thank you, Greg, for sharing your story of God's amazing grace. I pray many would read and be blessed and that many would read and come to a saving faith in Jesus Christ.

ED STETZER, executive director of the Wheaton College Billy Graham Center

Unlikely Fighter is a page-turner. If I didn't know Greg personally, I'd be tempted to think these stories were made up. But they're real. And they collectively make one powerful point: *the power of God can change anyone.* If you don't think God can change you, I dare you to read this book with an open heart.

SEAN MCDOWELL, PhD, associate professor of apologetics at Biola University and the coauthor of *Evidence That Demands a Verdict*

When you meet my friend Greg, instantly you will experience two things: he loves Jesus, and he loves for others to love Jesus. The love of Jesus pulsates in his body like electricity. And when you read *Unlikely Fighter*, that same electric volt will captivate your heart. This book is going to make you laugh out loud, it is going to make you cry. But above all, your passion for Jesus and his love for the world will be ignited!

DR. DERWIN L. GRAY, lead pastor of Transformation Church and the author of *God, Do You Hear Me?: Discover the Prayer God Always Answers*

For anyone who doesn't feel qualified to share the story of Jesus, this book is for you. You are more qualified than you know. With vulnerability, humor, and a genuine, unashamed love for the lost, Greg powerfully demonstrates how God uses the unlikely to reveal his love. Thank you, Greg, for equipping and empowering a generation to know Jesus and share the gospel.

HOSANNA WONG, international speaker, spoken word artist, and author of *How (Not) to Save the World*

Greg is a powerful communicator of the gospel to the next generation. I've heard some of the shocking stories from his violent upbringing woven into his sermons, but this book paints a much clearer picture of the often terrifying yet ultimately triumphant upbringing that Greg endured. This book is a powerful display that the gospel is "the power of God for the salvation of everyone who believes" . . . even for a family like Greg's.

DOUG FIELDS, author, speaker, and youth pastor

Beyond the brawls, bruises, and blood splattered across the pages of this hard-to-put-down book is the story of a scared, scarred little kid on a journey to find his identity. You will find yourself cheering, like I did, for the victory he, and eventually his entire family, found in Jesus.

SAMUEL RODRIGUEZ, pastor of New Season Church and president of the National Hispanic Christian Leadership Conference

This book is wild! Full of larger-than-life characters, divine encounters, authentic brokenness, and miraculous intervention and reconciliation! And it's all true. If Greg offers us one thing, it's hope—hope that the most unlikely and undeserving of us can find the way of life through the radical love of Jesus. This book will unleash a longing in you to be part of the wild adventure of God's Kingdom come!

DANIELLE STRICKLAND, author, advocate, and speaker

Listen, I want to be a part of anything Greg Stier does. He is always a blessing, and you'll be blessed by his new book, *Unlikely Fighter*! It's his personal story of God working in his life. You'll love the way he tells his story, and you'll feel like you're right there with him. It's real and unfiltered. But most importantly, it isn't just any story—it's a testimony of redemption, how God is mighty to save. Be sure to read this for yourself, and gift a copy to a young person!

SHANE PRUITT, national Next Gen evangelism director for North American Mission Board and author of *9 Common Lies Christians Believe*

Greg Stier is the genuine article, and his life is evidence of God's transforming power. If you've given up on yourself, take a page out of Greg's book. The gospel can change anything, change anyone.

MARK BATTERSON, *New York Times* bestselling author of *The Circle Maker* and lead pastor of National Community Church

I resonated deeply with Greg Stier's amazing testimony. As someone whose own upbringing was highly dysfunctional, I never cease to be amazed by the Lord's incredible grace in reaching down and placing his tender hand upon children surrounded by violence and brokenness. The story of how God's mercy brought salvation to Greg and each of his family members is something that will stay with you for a long time.

JIM DALY, president of Focus on the Family

In the '70s, I grew up in the same North Denver neighborhood as Greg, and in the early '80s, we became best friends while attending the same small fundamentalist Christian school. His intelligence, sharp wit, and spiritual passion were evident even back then. From his fatherless upbringing, to the shocking violence he witnessed as a child, to the dramatic conversation of his entire family, this book gave me a greater appreciation and understanding of Greg's early life experience and how that helped shape him into such a dynamically driven and influential adult.

SCOTT DERRICKSON, film director, screenwriter, and producer

GREG STIER

UNLIKELY

The Story of How a Fatherless Street Kid Overcame Violence,

Chaos & Confusion to Become a Radical Christ Follower

FIGHTER

TYNDALE
MOMENTUM®

A Tyndale nonfiction imprint

Visit Tyndale online at tyndale.com.

Visit Tyndale Momentum online at tyndalemomentum.com.

Tyndale, Tyndale's quill logo, *Tyndale Momentum*, and the Tyndale Momentum logo are registered trademarks of Tyndale House Ministries. Tyndale Momentum is the nonfiction imprint of Tyndale House Publishers, Carol Stream, Illinois.

Unlikely Fighter: The Story of How a Fatherless Street Kid Overcame Violence, Chaos, and Confusion to Become a Radical Christ Follower

Designed by Dean H. Renninger

Edited by Jonathan Schindler

Published in association with Don Gates of the literary agency The Gates Group; www.the-gates-group.com.

For information about special discounts for bulk purchases, please contact Tyndale House Publishers at csresponse@tyndale.com, or call 1-855-277-9400.

Library of Congress Cataloging-in-Publication Data

A catalog record for this book is available from the Library of Congress.

ISBN 978-1-4964-5155-2

Printed in the United States of America

27	26	25	24	23	22
7	6	5	4	3	2

To my ma, who loved me

in spite of her shame

CONTENTS

FOREWORD

I'VE GOTTEN TO KNOW a lot of extraordinary people through the years, but Greg Stier is among my very favorites. When we first met, we instantly felt a special affinity. We shared a mutual passion for telling as many people as possible about Jesus. In short, our hearts beat in unison for seeing lives and eternities transformed by Christ.

As I've gotten to know Greg better, though, I've come to realize there's another commonality that binds us together: both of us are unlikely fighters.

Three thousand years ago, a shepherd boy named David—armed with nothing more than a sling and a stone—successfully took on a nine-foot-six warrior, thanks to God's guiding hand. Similarly, Greg and I have faced and fought our own giants that were simply too big and imposing for us to defeat on our own.

For me, the battle was against the skepticism that propelled me down the path of atheism. My cynical self-interest convinced me there was no God and therefore anything was permissible. That resulted in a life of hedonism that deeply hurt my family and me.

It wasn't until my agnostic wife's conversion to Christianity that I used my journalism and legal training in a quest to disprove her faith—only to become persuaded by the evidence that Jesus is the unique Son of God who proved his divinity by returning from the dead.

As for Greg, he wrestled with his personal identity. As an almost-aborted, fatherless teen from the inner city, surrounded by a violence-prone family (with the biceps to back it up), Greg fought throughout his childhood and teen years to find out who he was, whose he was, and why he was.

Greg's life was on a downward spiral until a series of unlikely events changed the trajectory of his life—and, ultimately, that of his entire family.

What I love about Greg is that he has continued fighting to this very day. Now he's battling the ultimate adversary, Satan himself, in order to help every last person have a chance to hear the same Good News that set Greg and his family free.

In this captivating and encouraging book, you'll read the fascinating details of Greg's rocky journey to Christ and his new mission to ignite a spiritual revival. In fact, Greg and I are now fighting for you—that is, every reader of this book—to have the same deep encounter with God that has changed everything for us and our families.

Because in a way, we're all unlikely fighters who are engaged in various struggles of our own. Whether it's spiritual skepticism (as it was for me), personal identity (as it was for Greg), or some other battle that you're waging, I want you to know that we're cheering you on.

And I'm betting that this book will give you a strong infusion of Holy Spirit–inspired courage to swing the sling, fling the stone, and topple the giant that's blocking your path to a life of hope, freedom, and unparalleled adventure through Christ.

Lee Strobel
Bestselling author of The Case for Christ

INTRODUCTION

THE APOSTLE PAUL called himself "the chief of sinners," but he had never met the members of my family. If he had, he may have had to forfeit his title.

I often start my sermons with the same two sentences: "I don't come from a typical churchgoing, pew-sitting, hymn-singing family. I come from a family filled with body-building, tobacco-chewing, beer-drinking thugs . . . and that's just the women."

After everyone laughs at the unexpected twist, I go on to tell some of the wild, teetering-on-unbelievable stories of my family upbringing. Sometimes I tell stories about my baseball-bat-wielding, shame-filled mom (who I always called Ma), or my fist-throwing, cop-choking Uncle Jack, or my beat-you-till-you-cry-or-die Uncle Bob.

But the stories I tell in this book always finish the same way, demonstrating that the power of God can change any person in any family from any background.

"Are those stories true?" is a question I usually get asked after I preach a sermon that includes some family stories.

"Yes, they are true" is the answer I always give.

Much of what I share in this book I've seen with my own eyes. The other stories have been corroborated by the eyewitness testimony of family and family friends, many of whom I've spent hours interviewing for this book.

And, just to prepare you, much of it is violent. As troubling as some of the stories were to write, it was exponentially more troubling to experience them as a scared kid. Although most of the violence was not against me, it impacted me deeply and left a mark on my soul that is still there to this day.

When writing a memoir, you depend on memories, your own and others', to get the facts straight. I've done my best to do just that in this book. But only God's Word is infallible and inerrant.

Before I was old enough to get my driver's license, I had seen more rage, more dysfunction, and more blood than most people will see their entire lives. It was every bit as dramatic and traumatic as you can imagine.

And I wouldn't change any of it because this is my story of rescue. Actually, it's my entire family's rescue story. God rescued us from our sins and ourselves, and the entire trajectory of our family has been forever altered.

I am so grateful for his grace and mercy toward us, the chiefs of sinners.

CHAPTER 1

"A BUM LIKE ME"

A TYPICAL WARM SPRING DAY IN DENVER—the sky clear, the air dry, and the sun bright. Saturdays were for cleaning. Although we were dirt poor, we weren't, in Ma's words, "dirty poor."

While she cleaned inside, I played outside, my yellow Tonka dump truck, a couple G.I. Joes, and an assortment of toy guns strewn across the porch. But on this particular Saturday, my yellow plastic Wiffle bat had my undivided attention. I loved hitting the harmless white Wiffle balls around—especially out on the street. I could slug them good and hard, then watch them soar through the air and roll and roll. When the bat connected with the ball, just for a moment, everything felt right in the universe. I imagined this might be what it felt like to be a typical kid in a typical family in a typical neighborhood.

I was trying to muster up the courage to ask Ma if I could take it out to the street to hit a few, even though I suspected she would say no. She didn't want me to stray too far from our run-down rental—one of those old, red-brick cracker-box duplexes built in the early 1900s for the working class. Over the decades, the working class had moved up and out of the neighborhood and passed off these dilapidated, two-bedroom sardine-cans to the poor.

As with "home base" when playing tag, I felt safe at home. Sure, we had our share of scares, but when my mom was there, I knew nobody could touch me. She was the ultimate mama bear, a mixture of a soccer mom and the Terminator—the Mominator.

Ma was a fighter. She'd been raised in a violent family. Her dad, who loaded hundred-pound bags of flour by hand day in and day out, was known to knock bad guys out with a single punch. Her brothers, all five of them, were as tough as they come—a uniquely violent crew made up of street fighters, soldiers, boxers, brawlers, martial artists, and take-you-apart-ists.

And Ma could brawl with the best of them. Although she was always told that she looked like a young Elizabeth Taylor, she had the punch of Chuck Norris.

But I don't want to paint the picture of my mom as a violent beast. She was the most generous person I have ever known. She had almost nothing, but would give her meager resources—money, clothes, food—to those around her in genuine need.

But if you were a jerk, she would jerk you back to reality—sometimes with a sudden yank, sometimes with a punch.

Ma was a one-of-a-kind combo—a strange mixture of generosity, honesty, and kindness combined with a hair-trigger temper and ready fists to back it up. I have never seen the likes of her anywhere. Like a cocktail mixed on a whim one night with a variety of ingredients you can't quite remember, Ma was special. And, like a cocktail, she came with a kick.

We lived in North Denver, which, in the 1970s, was "the bad part of town." Sirens were no stranger to our neighborhood—or to our house. The neighborhood was a tinderbox of racial tension between the Italians and the Latinos. Shouting matches, fights, gunshots, and knifings were common.

Ma was terrified that trouble would find me someday without her around to protect me. She knew I really wasn't a fighter—not *that* kind of fighter, anyway. I was a quiet kid who loved books. And book-loving kids didn't fare well in our neighborhood.

Maybe that's why Ma relentlessly reminded me of the dangers lurking out there on the streets for little boys who wandered away from home alone. Ma would warn me about the predators in the park. "They'll snag you off the jungle gym, and you'll never be seen again," she threatened. There were molesters at the mall, too. "Stay by my side the whole time, or they'll grab you and run," she cautioned. And there were stalkers in the street. "They're just waiting for the right time to throw you in their van and speed away."

Ma was truly afraid that some really bad stuff could happen to me in our crime-infested neighborhood. Giving me all these worst-case scenarios was her way of trying to make me street smart.

On that spring day in Denver, I knew the chances of her letting me hit Wiffle balls in the street without my older brother, Doug, or one of my scrappy, street-smart older cousins was slim.

As I gazed out to the street longingly, a brand-new car slowly pulled up to the curb. It caught my attention not only because it was right in front of me but because the car was so shiny and clean—a real rarity in our neighborhood.

What really caught my attention was the man in the driver's seat. After he parked the car, he just sat there. He was strangely still, gripping the steering wheel. Seconds passed, but he just sat there with the car running.

Is this one of the "bad guys" Ma is always warning me about? I strained my eyes to see if I could catch a glimpse of his face. A flash of familiarity swept over me.

It was Paul—my stepdad. Ma had married him just a few months earlier. I don't remember a wedding. I don't even remember them dating. Maybe it was one of those spur-of-the-moment weddings.

Paul was different from the kind of men Ma usually attracted. She was typically surrounded by "manly" men, men covered in tattoos, back when tats were a sign that you had been in the armed forces or prison or both. Paul, on the other hand, always wore a white short-sleeved button-up shirt and tie to work. I had no clue what he did for a living, but I was impressed that he got dressed up to go to work. Perhaps Paul was Ma's shot at respectability.

But Paul, just like the other men who had been in her life, just wasn't working out. And he knew it.

One day, out of the blue, he just disappeared. He packed up his stuff while Ma was at work and left us. She came home, and he was gone. Poof. No note, no phone call, no Paul.

We had no idea where he went.

For days Ma had been mumbling under her breath, between

cigarette puffs, while washing dishes or cleaning up around the house, "Paul, that jerk! If he ever comes back here, I'm gonna mess him up." And she meant it. And she could.

Ma was no stranger to violence. Her five brawling brothers all had a healthy respect for their fighting sister. My toughest uncle, Uncle Jack, once asked me, "Do you wanna know the secret to beating your mom in a fistfight?"

"Not really," I'd said. But he told me anyway. "You gotta fight her like she's a dude!"

That's how I knew that Ma was really tough. If my bodybuilding, street-fighting, madman Uncle Jack—the toughest guy I'd ever met—was proud that he could beat my mom in a fistfight, Ma was one tough customer.

On that hot summer day, Paul should have known better than to show up for a face-off with Ma. Maybe that was why he was still sitting there frozen to his steering wheel, car still running.

After watching Paul just sitting there for a minute or so, I decided it was time to do something. I stepped inside the front door and yelled, "Ma! Ma! Paul's here!"

Ma looked out the front window, and her face erupted in rage. "Paul!" she yelled, cursing and calling him names. Then she desperately started looking around the room, yelling, "Where's that baseball bat?"

In my five-year-old innocence, I raised my yellow Wiffle bat and said, "Here, Ma!" But she didn't want the Wiffle bat. She wanted the Louisville Slugger, the real wooden bat that we kept behind the front door in case of intruders.

She grabbed the wooden bat in a flash and dashed outside, down the front steps, and straight toward his car. Curious, I followed her. I heard more curse words in that twenty-yard run than I'd ever heard in my life.

When she reached the car, Ma raised the baseball bat and began to relentlessly pound Paul's nice new car. She started with the headlights. Then she bashed in his front windshield, took out his driver's side mirror, and started doing body damage, cussing like a sailor with each blow and daring him to get out of the car.

He was still strangely still, almost mannequin-like as he sat there, gripping the steering wheel. No doubt he was wondering, *Should I just drive off, or should I try to stop her?*

Paul should have just driven off. But instead, he made the tactical mistake of getting out of the car. That's when the bat started *really* doing damage. Ma lit him up good. She turned the bat into a battering ram and jammed the top of the bat straight into his nose at full force. His nose exploded like a blood grenade. And then she started beating him relentlessly. Paul screamed with each blow she landed. Although I expected him to hightail it back into his car and speed away, instead he headed toward the house. Petrified, I watched in horror.

Doing his best to dodge Ma's vicious swings, Paul stumbled through the front door, made a beeline for the spot where Ma kept the most recent mail, and grabbed the entire pile—letters, junk mail, everything. Pieces of mail fell to the ground as Ma continued to chase him in the house and back out the front door.

Paul had come for the tax return check. And although he'd managed to retrieve it on that fateful Saturday, a few days later Ma had my uncle Bob track Paul down and forcibly collect it from him. To Ma's great satisfaction, Uncle Bob reported with a smile on his face that Paul was still black and blue from Ma's beating.

Ma slipped Uncle Bob a hard-earned hundred-dollar bill for his trouble.

There are certain memories that are seared in your mind with the hot iron of adrenaline and fear. The sight of Ma walking back up that sidewalk with a splintered, bloodied bat in one hand and a cigarette still hanging out of her mouth is one I'll never forget.

Paul wasn't the first man who had disrespected Ma and triggered a volcanic eruption of the Hulk-like rage that simmered just beneath the surface. She had a long history of looking for love in all the wrong places. By the time I was five, she had already been married a few times and had been with many men.

Ma loved to party. She worked hard during the day and partied hard at night. Friday nights, and sometimes Saturday nights, she'd go dancing at the Shangri La, leaving me and my big brother at home alone.

Doug and I would not wait up for her because she would usually come home after one or two in the morning. She told me once that her favorite dance partner was a member of the mob. He was so strong, he could lift her to the ceiling with one hand. According to Ma, "He was a monster in the streets but Fred Astaire on the dance floor."

Ma's hard partying resulted in a long string of short-term relationships that inevitably ended badly. Whenever the newest guy left her, or cheated on her, or put her down, she reacted violently because she felt disrespected.

"All men are jerks!" she would say after each breakup.

"But Ma," I would reply, "I'm going to grow up to be a man. I won't be a jerk."

"You're right! You won't grow up to be jerk. I won't take no disrespect from my boys."

And she didn't. Like many parents of her day, Ma firmly believed in using corporal punishment, especially when we were disrespectful to her. You didn't need to dare her to discipline. It was second nature to her. Ma often delivered her spankings with a flare all her own.

Once I saw Paul take his beating at her hands, Ma's rage-o-meter left me wondering when she might explode next. I knew I didn't want to be within slapping distance when she blew.

In one memorable instance, it was my brother, Doug, who set off Ma's temper.

Once in a great while, Ma would scrape enough money together to take my brother and me out to a sit-down restaurant. One of her favorite places was a family-friendly, dingy little diner just off Federal Boulevard called Chuck Wagon.

That particular day, my brother ordered a larger, more expensive meal than normal. This made Ma a little mad to begin with. Then suddenly, he wasn't hungry. This made her even madder.

She bluntly commanded him, "You eat all of your food, Doug. Don't just sit there and look at it." Ma was serious. We didn't eat out often, and when we did, she wanted every last scrap of food cleaned off our plates.

While I was only five, my brother was twelve years old, and he was feeling his about-to-be-a-teenager rebellious streak.

"Well, I'm not hungry anymore!" Doug exclaimed.

She leaned over to him, which was never a good sign, and said in her deep, raspy smoker's voice, "Listen to me, boy. You're going to eat every scrap of food on your plate."

To my surprise, my brother folded his arms and declared, "No, I'm not. I'm not hungry."

Ma never threatened; she prophesied. She leaned in even closer and declared, "If you don't start eating your food right now, I'm going to take you outside to the middle of the street and beat your bare bottom in front of God and everyone."

All during this time, I was quietly eating my food, watching the action. This was better than sitting in Ma's red Pinto watching cops fight criminals on Friday night, which we sometimes did for entertainment. But I didn't have to wonder who would win this showdown. I was just waiting to see if Doug would cave and obey in time to save his hide.

But Doug doubled down. He clenched his jaw and said between gritted teeth, "You will not."

In a flash, Ma jumped up from her chair and grabbed him by the arm. Then, with Doug screaming every step of the way, she dragged him outside. I just sat in my chair, eating my food—all of it. Five minutes later Doug came back in, tears streaming down his face. He sat down and quietly ate all his food too.

Later that day, Doug told me what happened. Ma had taken him outside, dragged him over to the median in the middle of the street, tore down his pants and underwear, and beat his bare bottom with her hand . . . in front of God and everyone.

Prophecy fulfilled.

He also added a juicy tidbit that made me wish I'd followed them outside to watch the action. During his public spanking, a lady who saw what was going on pulled her car over, got out, and marched up to Ma to try to stop her. When she got a few feet away, Ma looked up from the spanking and growled at the well-meaning woman, "Lady, if you come one step closer, I'll pull down your pants and spank you, too."

And Ma would have.

The lady pivoted back to her car, got in, and drove away.

Today, my mom would have been jailed for pulling such a stunt, and my brother and I would have been sent to child protective services. But back in the early '70s, laws weren't so rigorously enforced, especially in our part of the city.

Between the swinging baseball bat and the public spanking, I knew to stay on Ma's good side. I'd seen her other side enough times to know I never wanted to be the object of her rage.

Ma had felt disrespected by men all her life, and she refused to be disrespected by her own sons. Of course, we knew that she loved us deeply, but this love was always tempered by a fuse so short it could smash noses, break driver's side mirrors, and leave bare bottoms red.

As a little kid, I sometimes wondered why she was so angry. And I also wondered why she would cry so often. Ma would frequently start crying before I went off to bed. With tears streaming down her face, she'd look at me or Doug and say, "I don't want you to end up being a bum like me!"

Night after night, whenever she began to cry, I would stand by her side, pat her back, and say, "Ma, I won't be a bum. Neither will Doug. And you're not a bum either."

But night after night she'd shake her head in protest and declare between sobs, "You have no idea the things I've done. I'm a bum. I'm a bum!"

When Ma cried, it was no quiet whimper. She would cry as loud as she'd curse. Ma was angry, and she was hurt. It wasn't just disrespect that fueled her rage. It was also guilt and shame.

As her nightly tears attested, Ma continually beat up on herself as much as or more than she beat up on those around her who lit her fuse.

Every tear she shed and every punch she threw came from a place of deep hurt and regret. When men disrespected her, they were simply pouring gasoline on the burning shame she already felt. She already thought she was a bum, and their mistreatment of her fanned that inner flame into a raging forest fire.

CHAPTER 2

THE CRAZY BROTHERS

"IT STARTED LIKE ANY OTHER DAY," Uncle Dave told us as the family gathered in my grandparents' living room after a big Sunday afternoon meal. "As usual, I was really hungry. Workin' out takes a steady stream of calories, ya know. I settled into a booth at this little Italian joint and could hardly wait for the plate of chicken and pasta. But when my food arrived, the chicken wasn't done.

"'Please send this chicken back to the cook, it ain't done,' I told the waitress. Firm, but nice, I was—the first time.

"'No problem, sir,' she says to me, as she took it away. But when the food came back, it was obvious the cook hadn't done a thing to it.

"'Send it back again. It still ain't done,' I says, but again, it came back undercooked. I began to suspect the cook was just toyin' with me.

"So, I sent it back a third time!" Uncle Dave exclaimed, pausing for dramatic effect. "That's when the mob underling who ran the place came stormin' out of the kitchen, dish in hand, and shoved the food down on the table in front of me. 'You don't like my chicken? You tryin' to start something here? 'Cause I have a gun, and we can figure this out.'

"So I just stood up, grabbed the dish, walked over to the trash can, and tipped the chicken and pasta plate to a full 90-degree angle and let the food slide off into the garbage. I looked straight in the eye of that Italian tough guy and said, 'Guess what? I got a gun too.'

"But just before it escalated any further, Checkers Smaldone —one of the higher-ups in the North Denver mob family— came over and told the cook, 'Hey, leave him alone! He's one of us!'"

Whenever Uncle Dave delivered this punch line to his story, he would let out a loud laugh and get a proud look on his face.

The Smaldones were the organized crime family who ruled the streets of North Denver in the '50s and '60s. Although they were not related to the five big mob families of New York City, this notorious Italian family ran a sizable bookmaking, gambling, racketeering, loansharking, and extortion operation. The Smaldones knew my uncles and gave them an endearing—and accurate—nickname: The Crazy Brothers.

When the mafia thinks your family is dysfunctional, you know you have problems.

Although my uncles—the Mathias brothers—were respected by the mob, they weren't members. They were more into disorganized crime than organized.

The Crazy Brothers weren't loan sharks, collectors, or drug

runners. They just loved violence. They craved it. It was their drug of choice. The adrenaline rush they got from defending their turf, their honor, and each other was a better high than any heroin or LSD they could buy on the street—it was free and readily available.

An unbridled rage was always bubbling just beneath the surface of my uncles' flexed facades, ready to lash out at anyone who crossed them. To add insult to the possibility of real bodily injury, the Mathias family was freakishly strong, built for fight, not flight.

These guys were always ready for a brawl. Yes, some of it was for the rush, but some of it was out of necessity. We lived in a part of the city that chewed up the weak and spit out the bones. We lived in a section of town that was rife with racial tension as well as crime.

North Denver had two primary neighborhoods, Italian and Mexican. The racism between these two groups was palpable, and it often spilled over into the streets. It may not have been *West Side Story*, but it definitely was the North Side's.

The Italians had established their place in North Denver in the mid-1800s during the heyday of the Colorado Gold Rush. There were so many Italians living in this part of the city, it was nicknamed "Little Italy."

But a century later, things were changing. People of Mexican descent began to move into North Denver. And with each new infusion of Latino blood into the neighborhood, the temperature of the tensions rose.

Denver, and specifically North Denver, was viewed by some as an epicenter of the "American Chicano Movement." Denver-based leaders like Corky Gonzales and Richard Castro launched

"The Crusade for Justice" that triggered boycotts, strikes, and riots in the battle for equal rights for Latinos. Mexican American activism and pride ran high.

But to the Italian Americans, already firmly established in North Denver, the Mexican Americans were seen more as invaders than neighbors. The Italians were bitter that the Latinos were moving into their beloved "Little Italy." The Latinos were miffed that the Italians didn't respect their culture and their rights as Americans to live where they wanted.

By the time I arrived on the scene in 1965, geographically, there were two North Denvers—North Side Mexican and North Side Italian. My family lived on the Mexican side of the geographic divide.

And because of where we lived, our family stood out and had to stand strong. Although my family was Welsh, we looked and acted Italian. And we, unlike so many others in our part of North Denver, refused to be pushed out by anyone.

My uncles were big and hard to budge anyway.

Three of them were competitive bodybuilders, and all of them loved the push, pull, lift, and grunt of the weight room. Long before Arnold Schwarzenegger ruled Gold's Gym, the exercise guru Jack LaLanne ruled the airwaves.

Exercise was about health, fitness, flexibility, and strength, not unnaturally big, drug-induced muscles. Steroids had not yet been injected into the bodybuilding scene. It was all about natural strains and gains. Aspiring bodybuilders strained their muscles in the gym and gained them back, and then some, in the kitchen.

The Crazy Brothers were early adopters of the weightlifting, bodybuilding culture. As a result, family gatherings were full of pose downs and showdowns.

Phrases like "check these babies out" and "take a look at these guns" would fly back and forth across the room like a medicine ball in a game of catch between Goliath's brothers. One uncle would flex his biceps or triceps or whatever-ceps in the direction of his testosterone-fueled brothers, and they would reciprocate with their own pose.

But their muscles weren't just for show; they were for go. They worked out for strength and power more than flash and flex. When they hit someone, they wanted it to rattle their ancestors.

Half the fun was the fight. The other half was telling and retelling the story of the fight to the rest of the family.

As a kid, one of my favorite things was listening to my uncles tell stories. And every funeral, wedding, and family reunion was an opportunity to hear them recount their fighting stories, some of which were in the distant past and others of which had just happened. From the time I was old enough to understand, I'd position myself as close as I could to the big table so I could hear their amazing exploits. They were like superheroes to me. Scary superheroes.

The adults pulled their chairs up around my grandparents' huge kitchen table, encircling it like a tribal campfire. We kids were relegated to silence in the nooks and crannies of the background. On this occasion, four of my five uncles were there, plus some new people who had just been introduced to the Mathias family. Fresh ears meant the best and bloodiest exploits would be shared. I scooted in closer, eager to absorb it all like a sponge.

Dave, the fourth of the five brothers, kicked off the storytelling time. His curly brown hair and tall physique combined to give him the look of a gunslinger in an old western. But when he spoke, he sounded like he was from Jersey, not Colorado.

Uncle Dave was a Golden Gloves boxer, as well as a black belt heavyweight judo champion. Dave fought in the streets even more than he did in the ring or on the mat. He was not a bodybuilder or powerlifter, but he could take you out just as quickly as my other uncles with a strong right hook or a judo choke hold.

Before he could launch into his first story, Uncle Bob threw out a prompt. "Tell these folks 'bout the time you got bayoneted!"

Dave looked down and stared intently at his strong, gnarled hands that lay folded in front of him on the table. A lot of his friends had died during the Vietnam War. He was the crew chief of a rescue helicopter, and he and his team went on a seemingly endless array of dangerous rescue missions. They would fly into hot zones where bullets and bombs were still flying so that they could rescue the wounded and load dead bodies onto their copter to ensure they received a proper burial.

After a moment, Dave pulled himself back to the present and launched into his story.

"We were flyin' into a hot zone, and as the chopper was landin', I saw an American soldier bein' taken into the jungle. As soon as we touched down, my boots hit the ground, and I ran into the dense jungle where they'd dragged him.

"Before I knew it, three Vietcong soldiers had tackled me, took my gun, and stood on me. Two guys stood on my arms, and one guy straddled me with his AK-47 and bayonet pointin' at my gut. These guys were laughin', 'cause they knew they had me.

"So this guy plunges the bayonet into my gut and starts cuttin' upward." Dave pulled his shirt up to show the five-inch gash in the middle of his stomach.

Our visitors gasped in horror. If they thought Dave had been stretching the truth up to this point, their doubts vanished. The jagged ugliness of the huge scar served as corroborating evidence.

"What did you do?" one of the visitors asked.

"I prayed to God and kicked him in the groin." The entire room burst into laughter. "It was the weirdest thing. Both soldiers jumped off my arms, and the guy I kicked dropped the gun. When he did, the gun spun out of his arms and landed perfectly into my now freed hands. So I shot him, killed the other two guys, rescued the American soldier, and flew another six hours after that."

"What about your gash?" someone asked.

"I duct-taped it. When my shift was over, I had the surgeon stitch it up," Dave explained.

Our guests sat in stunned silence for a moment until Bob broke it by launching into the next story. "Yeah, Dave could handle himself," Bob said admiringly. "We all could handle ourselves."

Uncle Bob was the baby of the group, but he was one big baby. At six foot three inches tall and north of 230 pounds, he was a beast who looked more like an offensive lineman than a bodybuilder. For decades, Bob worked as a pipe fitter and regularly lifted 500-pound pipes as part of his job. He had brute natural strength that other men coveted. As a bouncer at one of the toughest bars in Denver, his fighting skills were honed on the meanest and strongest bad guys in the city.

But that night, Bob didn't talk about himself. Instead, he bragged on his absent brother, the second oldest, Richard. "What always surprised everyone was what a good brawler Richard was," Bob said, by way of introduction.

Uncle Richard was a bodybuilder, street fighter, and entre-preneur. Nicknamed "Elvis" by some, he was the most suave and handsome of the Crazy Brothers. Unlike most of my family, Richard had a knack for making money. Long before I was born, he'd moved to Phoenix to start his own business and make his fortune. But despite his good looks and money-making skills, Richard could throw fists with the best of them.

"Do you remember that night when a group of gang members who knew where we lived drove down the alley right next to the house on Irving Street callin' us out?" Bob asked the brothers, glancing around the table.

"Which time?" Uncle Jack yelled. Howls of laughter erupted.

"The time when Richard screamed 'Fight!' and ran out the door, chargin' full speed toward that car." It was obvious by the looks on their faces that they not only remembered the situation but were reliving it with relish as Bob retold it.

Bob continued. "That crazy Richard dove headfirst through the open car window, totally shockin' 'em."

"That's Richard!" Uncle Jack bellowed. "He surprised everyone with how tough he was. And once he got in the car, he punched and kicked at everyone he could . . . and they punched him back!"

Commandeering the story back from Jack, Bob continued. "It must have shocked them, though, because they squealed their tires out of the alley and onto the street. They sped away, but Richard must have grabbed the steering wheel and jerked it a few times."

"Yeah," Dave joined in, "that car swerved and weaved until it finally banked right and hit a parked car."

"Then we all ran down the street," Jack said, taking over again, "and pulled those suckers out of the car and beat 'em."

Uncle Tommy, the oldest, least violent, and most respected of the uncles, looked directly at me—which was a rarity, since my uncles seldom acknowledged a child in their midst—and added, "Your mom, not one to be left out, grabbed her baseball bat and, in nothing but a bathrobe, sprinted down the street and joined in the fun, too. Do you remember that, Shirley?"

"You bet I do," Ma shot back, sending a stream of cigarette smoke across the table.

While Tommy could fight too, he generally preferred not to. At his core, he had a gentler soul than the rest of my uncles. He would rather be a peacemaker than a jawbreaker. Perhaps it was because he was the most secure of the group. He had won the most bodybuilding awards, and as the oldest and most mature, he had nothing to prove. But that didn't keep him from admiring the fighting spirit in his siblings. Turning back toward me again, Tommy told me something I already knew. "Your mama sure can fight."

The brothers howled in agreement.

Jack finished the story. "We beat those guys until the cops showed up," he said. "Thank God they were all wanted."

"Yeah," Bob shot back. "That was one of the few times the cops showed up and you didn't get arrested, right, Jack?"

"Right!" Jack said with a laugh.

In a family full of black sheep, Uncle Jack was the blackest, the meanest, and the most volatile. Like Ma, down deep he had a generous heart, but unlike her, he wasn't just ready for a fight, he was looking for one.

Jack looked like a beefed-up version of the Marvel Comics

character nicknamed the Wolverine. The long lambchop side-burns that grew down his square jaw met his Fu Manchu mustache at the ends of his snarling lips. Even his shaving habits gave him the look of a man not to be trifled with. But more than his facial hair, his oversized biceps and forearms, covered in jailhouse green tattoos, ranged in design from a rattlesnake coming out of a skull to a flying eagle.

Jack went to jail a lot in his younger years. The family sometimes speculated that he would have been even more prone to violence and criminal activity if he hadn't met and fallen in love with his wife, Earlene. Once, when Jack was asked to describe his early years of continual run-ins with the law, he explained it like this: "I was born on skid row in Denver. I lived in jail in the fifties. When I met Earlene, I was on an indefinite sentence of probation. I introduced Earlene to my probation officer. He says, 'Gosh, Jack, that's the only *good* girl I ever seen you run with. When are you going to get married?' I says, 'Not until you let me off this probation.' He says, 'You're off.' I've been married to her ever since."[1]

But even with Earlene in his life, Jack went way farther than even the toughest guys typically dared. As a kid, I heard story after story of Jack's violent outbursts.

Like the warm summer night he and Earlene went to Lakeside, an old-style amusement park just north of our neighborhood. The way Earlene told me the story, Jack had just bought her a new coat.

"Thank you for the coat, Jack! I love it!" she said, wearing it with pride that night, despite the July heat.

---

[1] S. K. Badgett, *Digging in the Dark: Tales from the Mines of Carbondale and Beyond* (Carbondale, CO: Globeflower Press, 2018), 52.

"I think I'll put some mustard on it to balance the colors out," Jack joked, pretending to squeeze the hotdog stand condiment bottle in her direction. My uncle may have been rough and tough, but he had a sweet and comical side to him as well. This usually came out when he was around Earlene.

Earlene beamed as she sported her prized coat, a treasured gift from the rough-around-the-edges, muscle-bound man she loved. But that changed when a passing tough guy hurled an insult her direction: "Nice coat! You idiot, don't you know it's July?"

Like a shark rolling its eyes into the back of its head when attacking, my relatives' eyes always darkened whenever their attack-mode switch was activated. All the members of my family seemed to have this switch. Ma had the switch. Jack had that switch. And when the switch flipped, it was over.

Jack's eyes turned black with rage. In a flash, he lunged at the guy and had him on the ground. Over and over, Jack pounded the guy's face, and with each punch of his huge fists, the back of the guy's head bounced against the concrete. Jack beat his face into mash.

The Lakeside cops on duty came running up to Jack and pushed him off the man. Realizing that this most likely meant more time in jail, Jack made a run for it. But my family is not built for running. So when the two police officers caught up to him, Jack pulled out his signature move and grabbed each of them by the throat—simultaneously, one in each hand.

Technically, it was their windpipes that he grabbed.

Jack had a fully developed philosophy about how to choke someone, which he loved explaining to me again and again. "When you choke a guy," he'd say, "never grab him around the full neck. There're too many muscles there that they can flex. And that'll keep you from chokin' 'em out. Instead, grab 'em by the windpipe, and grab 'em hard. You can cut off their air completely and, if you do it right, they'll black out in seconds."

The two cops never had a chance. But reinforcements were close behind. When the other police officers arrived on the scene, they whipped out their billy clubs and beat Jack senseless. Then they arrested him.

So much for a fun night at the amusement park. Instead, Jack spent the night in jail.

When Jack and Earlene finally had kids, it seemed like a ray of hope might finally be shining through. Jack adored his two daughters, Tammy and Jackie. Out of all the things he had screwed up in his life, his girls seemed to be turning out all right. Still, his propensity to violence was always there, like a tiger ready to pounce at the slightest provocation. He sensed that it was only a matter of time before another violent outburst landed him in jail . . . once again.

But as Uncle Jack told us later, all of that changed the day a man nicknamed "Yankee" rang his doorbell.

CHAPTER 3

THE KNOCKOUT BLOW

ONE SUNDAY AFTERNOON Uncle Jack and Aunt Earlene invited Ma, Doug, and me over to their place. Jack said he had something important he wanted to tell Ma about. Grandma was there too. As Jack recounted the story, Aunt Earlene passed beers around to the adults while Grandma poured big glasses of lemonade for us kids. It was the first time I heard the story that Jack would tell and retell to anyone who would listen.

Jack told us that he was watching TV and drinking a beer when the doorbell rang and Lobo went crazy. Lobo was their gigantic German shepherd. He was a puppy dog if he knew you, all wagging tail and big licks, but if he didn't know you, he was a nightmare waiting to pounce, all raised hair and bared teeth. He greeted every stranger who came to the door by planting his big front paws up on the screen door so he was snout-to-face with whoever came knocking.

As usual, Earlene grabbed Lobo's collar and dragged him to the back room while Jack headed for the door to see what was what. He was shirtless, with two beer cans in hand—one for drinking beer and one for spitting chew.

He was flexed up and ticked off that somebody was interrupting them on a Saturday morning.

"Whaddya want?" Jack barked through the screen. He was suspicious because the man on the other side was wearing a suit and tie. But the stranger was calm and collected, as if neither Lobo nor Jack barking at him had set his ears back one bit.

"Good morning," the man said. "My name is Pastor Yankee Arnold." Jack thought this was strange, because while the guy had a deep Southern drawl, he called himself Yankee.

"Your daughters are going to youth group at my church," Yankee continued, "and I just want to tell you what sharp, beautiful girls they are. As a dad, you must be so proud." That was just about the only thing Yankee could have said to get Jack to open the door. Since Yankee complimented his girls, that was enough for him. So Jack invited him in.

After a little more small talk, Yankee cut to the chase and said, "I have a question for you."

"Shoot," Jack said back.

"Do you know for sure you're going to heaven when you die?"

Jack responded with the first thing that came into his head. "I know for sure I'm going to hell!"

Since Grandma and Grandpa had dragged their kids to church every week when they were little, Jack knew all about sin and hell, and he knew he was full of one and headed to the other. All that hellfire and brimstone at church just made him feel bad about himself, while friends and partying and fighting made him feel good. He still believed in God, but he wasn't sure God believed in him anymore. He was sure that with all the things he'd done wrong and the anger he had inside, he was on the highway to hell.

But Yankee asked him, "If I could tell you how you could know for sure that you were going to heaven, would that be good news?"

Jack appreciated Yankee's bluntness. His question was almost like a punch to the gut. Jack was surprised by how quickly he said yes.

Emboldened by Jack's answer, Yankee drew his wallet from his back pocket and launched into an illustration he'd nicknamed "The Hand Gesture."

"Let this hand represent you and me," Yankee said, holding up his own right hand in the air. "And let this hand represent God." Yankee held up his left hand. "And let the wallet represent sin. Have you ever sinned?" Yankee asked, already knowing the answer.

"Yes!" Jack told him.

"Well, we all have," Yankee said, putting the wallet in his right hand. "Remember, this hand with the wallet in it here, this represents us." He waved his right hand with the wallet in it back and forth a little.

"You see," Yankee continued, "God loves us, but he hates our sin, because that sin is a barrier between us and him." Yankee joined his hands together in a praying-hands formation with the wallet in between them. "And, as a result of that sin, we are all condemned to hell forever."

Jack had never been much for book-learning or sermon-listening, but Yankee's wallet illustration made sense to him.

"And no matter how good you are, it will never get rid of these sins," Yankee told Jack. Then Yankee picked up his big black Bible and held it over the wallet. "If this Bible represents everything good we do, does it get rid of the sin or just cover it up?"

"It just covers it up," Jack said.

"So religious people still sin, right?" Yankee asked.

"Sure," Jack said.

"And because of that sin, they're condemned to hell along with everyone else. Right?"

"Yeah, I guess so," Jack responded. He was a little disoriented because he had never heard it explained like this before.

"So, two thousand years ago, God sent his Son, Jesus, into the world," Yankee explained, bringing his left hand, representing God, down toward the wallet. "Jesus was God in the flesh. He lived the perfect life we could never live and died the horrible death that we deserved. And when he died, he took our sin upon himself and paid the price for it with his own blood." Yankee plucked the wallet representing sin out of his right hand.

Then Yankee delivered the punchline. "Because Jesus took our sin upon himself and paid the price for it, if you simply believe that he did that for you and trust in him alone to forgive you for your sins, you will receive eternal life."

Jack was silent at this point, so Yankee continued, testing Jack. "How long is eternal life?" Yankee asked.

"It's forever!" Jack told him with a tone of raw excitement, because Jesus' message was making sense to him for the very first time in his life.

"So, if you trust in Jesus right now, where will you go when you die?" Yankee asked.

"Heaven!" Jack shouted back at him.

And then like a boxer who has been softening up his opponent with an endless string of jabs before delivering the knockout blow, Yankee asked Jack one final question. Looking him straight in the eyes, he asked, "So, if all of this makes sense, will you put your faith in Jesus to forgive you for all your sins and give you eternal life right now?"

"Hell, yeah!" Jack announced with a big smile on his face.

Then Yankee turned to Earlene and asked her the same question. And she trusted in Jesus, too!

In that moment, the trajectory of Jack and Earlene's life changed forever.

In the midst of hearing this story, Ma had pushed her chair back from the table, stood up abruptly, and walked out of the room. She'd had an upset look on her face, though I couldn't imagine why at the time. I thought it was a good story. Grandma did too—I could tell.

Still, I didn't fully understand the gospel yet at six years of age. I wasn't super concerned about it either. Death had not visited my doorstep yet—that I knew of anyway—so "going to heaven" seemed a long way off.

Years later, I learned that Jack had no idea that his two teenage daughters had repeatedly begged Yankee to go to their house and share the gospel with their mom and dad. My streetwise cousins, Tammy and Jackie, had warned Yankee how tough their dad was, but they loved their parents and wanted them to hear the gospel and have their lives transformed by Jesus, the way theirs had been.

Jack also had no idea that his old friend, Bob Daly, was sitting outside in Yankee's car. Bob was a longtime friend of the Mathias family and had gone to North High School with my uncles. Bob's life had been transformed by Yankee's ministry as well, and he, too, wanted Jack to hear about Jesus. So he had dared Yankee to tell Jack, and Yankee had taken that dare. But Bob stayed in the car and prayed while Yankee went inside to do the talking.

Years later, I better understood why my ma had bailed out of the conversation early. She was freaked out by the possibility that this Jesus could save a bum like her.

But my grandma was thrilled by the story Jack told that day. Jack was still rough and tough, but now that he had Jesus, Grandma knew that Jesus would ultimately win any arm-wrestling match between Jack's old self and his new self. Still, she knew it would be messy, just as her story had been messy too.

CHAPTER 4

GRANNY'S GOT A GUN

EVERY SUPERHERO has an origin story. And my superheroes—
my legendary uncles and my ma—had an origin story too.

Grandpa was the only one of his brothers and sisters born
in America. He was short and stocky. His skin was so dark and
olive-colored that he looked like one of those Italian mafiosos,
which is probably why everyone in the neighborhood thought
our family was Italian. But Grandpa was a Welsh man through
and through.

While his brothers were all coal miners, Grandpa worked at
a flour mill. He had the forearms of the old cartoon character
Popeye and a big barrel chest. His fingers were so thick he
couldn't fit a ring on them, and when he curled those fingers
into a fist, they became a sledgehammer.

Grandpa never worked out, but he was naturally strong—freakishly strong. He was the only guy at his flour mill who could take two one-hundred-pound bags of flour, one in each hand, and fling them onto each shoulder simultaneously like they were a couple of kindergarteners' school backpacks.

Unlike my ma and my uncles, Grandpa was quiet. But we all knew his quiet strength could turn violent at the drop of a hat. Even though Grandpa and Grandma were weekly churchgoing Baptists, Grandpa's hair-trigger temper frequently got the better of him. Relatively minor grievances easily erupted into full-blown violence.

There was a legendary family story from long before I was born that captured the paradox of my grandpa's churchgoing ways and his unbridled temper. It was one of those favorite stories my uncles loved to tell and retell when they gathered around the kitchen table at my grandparents' house.

"It was a warm, sunny Sunday afternoon," Uncle Dave was recounting. "We were in the car after church—Ma and Dad took us to Bethany Baptist every Sunday to give us some religion. I was twelve at the time, and Bob was eight."

"They took us to church, but it didn't take . . . for most of us, anyway," Uncle Bob interjected, with a dismissive laugh.

"Mom and Dad were in the front seat, and us kids were in the back of the family station wagon," Dave continued.

"We were on our way to Luby's Lakeside Cafeteria to eat lunch," Bob said, trying to hijack the story again. "The one at Lakeside Mall. Dad must have been drivin' slow or somethin', 'cause this guy races his car up next to us, flips Dad off, and starts cussin' him out through the open car windows."

"The guy pulls into the parking lot and parks his car, and

Dad pulls up right behind him," Dave said, taking control of the story again. "Dad gets out of the car, hands his fedora to Mom, and walks up to the driver's side of the guy's car. This poor guy, who was still sittin' in his car, probably wasn't the least bit worried about this guy who was all dressed up in his Sunday best with a station wagon full of kids.

"So, the guy makes a wisecrack to Dad. And all of a sudden, Dad grabs him through the open car window by the shirt with his left hand, pulls his head just out the window, and smashes him with a short right hook. He hit the guy so hard he flew all the way across the front seat and shattered the passenger's side window with his skull!"

"Clean across the front seat!" Bob emphasized. "Knocked him out cold with one punch!"

"I ain't ever seen anything like that since. Clean across the front seat!" Dave said, shaking his head in admiration as he relived the vivid memory from his childhood.

"When Dad got back in the car, nobody said a word," Bob continued. "We just looked at each other in stunned silence. Then we went into Luby's Cafeteria and ate our Sunday lunch like nothin' had happened."

"None of us ever doubted Dad's strength after that," Dave said. "In fact, if anything, it probably motivated all of us boys to want to grow up to be strong like him. That's probably why we all worked out so hard. Dad came by his strength naturally from his work at the mill, but we had to build our muscles by pumpin' iron at the gym."

Even as a kid, I found this story confusing. How could Sunday churchgoing and such explosive anger settle in side by side? But even though violence and the quest for God made for strange bedfellows, both had taken up residence in my grand-parents' home.

While my grandpa set the standard for strength in the family, it was Grandma who set the standard for toughness.

For as long as I can remember, I knew Grandma was tough. She kept both gum and a gun in her purse.

But what made Grandma unique was that she was, in many ways, a traditional, typical grandma. She loved family gatherings and made fudge for everyone at Christmastime. Being the mom to five boys and my ma, she knew how to cook for her large, perpetually hungry family. Plus, she was a first-class storyteller. My uncles learned the art of skillfully regaling a crowd with a suspense-filled story from her. And she loved to laugh, always giggling a distinctive, "Oh, gosh!" at the end of her frequent spasms of laughter.

Unlike her husband, Grandma wasn't physically intimidating in the slightest. She was a bit overweight and suffered from heart problems for decades, but those challenges didn't keep her down. Anyone who crossed her reaped the whirlwind. And she didn't pack that gun in her purse just for show. She knew how to use it and didn't hesitate to do so.

One particular incident that occurred up in the Rocky Mountains of Colorado was seared into my memory with crystal clarity.

The smell of the pine trees and damp earth filled the air. The clear, cobalt-blue sky dazzled my city-kid eyes. The mountain air was cool and crisp. I was in heaven! Camping with my grandparents was the highlight of every summer.

Grandpa and I would fish while Grandma stayed at the campsite, puttering around with food preparations so she'd be ready whenever we returned with our fishing trophies and tales of the big one that got away. Fishing was actually kind of boring for me because I had to keep quiet so I didn't "scare the fish away," but I enjoyed being with Grandpa. Throughout the course of an entire day of fishing in a sparkling mountain river, Grandpa might only speak three sentences to me, but it didn't matter. As a kid who had no dad at home, Grandpa was my only father figure—and I was in awe of him.

On this particular day, we were fishing half a mile or so away from our campsite when we heard a couple of gunshots. The sound of gunfire wasn't too out of the ordinary in the mountains of Colorado. But by the time we made our way back to camp, Grandma had quite a story to tell us.

"Didn't I tell you I smelled trouble!" Grandma said with a knowing toss of her head toward the now-empty campsite near ours. "I knew that passel of loud, rowdy, long-haired hippies causing all that commotion last night were up to no good.

"Well, I'll tell you what, they bit off more than they could chew when they made the mistake of threatenin' me! They had the gall to walk up to the edge of our camp and say, 'Hey lady, we're comin' through your camp to grab a few things.'

"Like I said," Grandma continued, "I smelled trouble from the start, so I had my .357 magnum revolver ready to go. So when they bragged that they needed a few things and were goin' to help themselves to what we had, I simply smiled and said, 'Just give it a try!' Then I lifted the pistol into the air for dramatic effect.

"The hooligans looked at each other, snickered, and came a few steps closer as the ringleader confidently boasted to the rest of them, 'Don't worry, the old lady doesn't even know how to use that thing.'

"So I fired a couple shots in the air to show them that I did. Then I lowered the gun toward the stunned ringleader and said, 'The next one's goin' right through your skull.'

"They packed up and hightailed it out of here in no time flat!" Grandma added with a laugh. "They're probably in the next county by now!"

Oddly enough, neither Grandpa nor I was the least bit surprised.

There were other stories too, like the time she shot a circle of bullets into the car door of two guys who tried to rob her. She fired her bullets into the shape of a circle so the police could easily identify the car and arrest the culprits.

Even in her later years, Grandma was feisty and refused to let anyone get the better of her. She kept her large key ring wrapped around her fingers to use like a poor man's brass knuckles if she ever needed to punch anyone. Once, when a thug attempted to mug her in a parking lot, instead of getting her purse, he got stitches. She was in her late seventies at the time.

Still, my favorite Grandma story as a kid had nothing to do with a gun but with a garden hose.

Old Miss Jay was our next-door neighbor during one of the times Ma, Doug, and I temporarily moved in with my grandparents at 22nd Avenue and Irving Street in North Denver. She was the kind of mean old lady who would just sit and look out her front window, waiting for one of the neighborhood kids' balls to accidentally land in her yard. Whenever a stray ball invaded her space, she would waddle her oversized frame outside, snag the ball, and add it to her collection. She was generally smart enough to avoid my grandma. Until one memorable day in July.

It was the hottest part of summer. Colorado's scorching sun and semi-arid climate left our lawn parched. So Grandma routinely watered the front lawn with a garden hose to keep it from shriveling up and dying. Our front yard was so small that Grandma had a system down where she could sit on her front porch while she watered the front grass. She used one of those spray nozzles that constricts the water into a powerful stream that could shoot all the way to the far corners of the yard.

I was sitting on the porch next to Grandma when old Miss Jay waddled across her front yard toward my grandma on a rampage. "I've had enough of your noisy grandkids!" she yelled at Grandma. "When they ride those Big Wheels up and down the sidewalk, they make a horrible racket. You need to keep those kids under control!"

Grandma just kept watering the front lawn as Miss Jay waddled closer and closer. When she finally got right next to our porch, Grandma turned the garden hose on her, full in the face. Shocked, the large lady let out a horrified scream, getting water in her mouth as she did. She hurriedly turned around and waddled back toward her own house as quickly as her massive frame would carry her. Grandma kept the hose on her the whole way, arcing the stream higher and higher to make sure Miss Jay was completely drenched before she escaped into the safety of her house.

Cool and collected, Grandma didn't say a word about it. She just turned the hose back on the front grass and watered away with a satisfied grin on her face.

Grandpa's freakish strength and Grandma's shocking toughness became the quiet standard for the Mathias family tribe. Behind every fistfight, bodybuilding competition, and arm-wrestling match there was the looming image of Grandpa and Grandma, strength and toughness combined. Each of their six children seemed to receive an equal mix of that DNA, as did most of their grandchildren.

But not me.

I didn't seem to fit into the family. I was not naturally strong or tough. I was a shy, insecure, bookish kid who used to try to find quiet places—under the sink or behind the couch—to read. Fighting someone was the last thing on my mind. Even when I started school at Brown Elementary as a first grader, I tried to avoid conflict. Kids would pick on me, and I would run away rather than stand and fight.

Halloween became one of my extended family's annual opportunities to toughen me up by bringing me into their shenanigans. They wanted to show me how to "break the rules," but in a way that wasn't dangerous—just mean.

There was a huge tree in front of Grandma and Grandpa's place on Irving Street. It had large branches that stretched like flexed, bark-covered arms over the front yard. The house itself was tailor-made for Halloween. Because it was built in the late 1800s from extra-large red bricks and old-school masonry, its narrow build shot to the sky like a spire and stood out from the other box houses in our neighborhood. Old Miss Jay's house was of the same construction and relatively close to our house, so at night, by the moonlight, our houses side by side looked like twin towers of terror.

Every year on Halloween, our extended family gathered for an exciting night of scaring the little kids in the neighborhood. Spooky music played from an upper-story window. One of my uncles volunteered to be the ghoul. The ghoul took off his shirt and donned a full-head scary mask. When neighborhood kids innocently rang the doorbell to trick-or-treat, the door flew open and the hulking ghoul shrieked out a monstrous roar.

Without exception, the poor, frightened kids turned and ran down the sidewalk toward the street to get away from our homemade insane asylum. That's when my brother and I kicked into action.

Each Halloween at dusk, we were instructed to climb the big tree in front of our house and wait. The uncles armed us with a life-size dummy that had a noose tied around its neck. Doug and I were told to tie the other end of the rope to the thick tree branch directly above the sidewalk that led to the front door. After the designated uncle ghoul scared the kids senseless on the porch, as the kids ran screaming down the sidewalk, our job was to drop the dummy out of the tree directly in front of them.

The plan was to terrorize the children so that they dropped their bags full of candy. And it worked about 50 percent of the time. My family got the biggest kick out of this annual Halloween ritual.

Crying kids ran home to tell their parents (back then, even in tough neighborhoods, moms and dads never went door-to-door with their children on Halloween), but no parent ever showed up at our house to complain. They knew who lived there. They knew what would happen if they dared to confront our family.

I hated dropping the dummy. I hated scaring those kids. Maybe it was because I related more to them in their fear than I did to my own family members. My experience of life in the middle of my chaotic, violent family felt a lot like those scared kids running from one terror to the next. But even though I hated the role I was forced to play in our annual Halloween drama, I did enjoy eating the dropped candy.

Still, Halloween didn't toughen me up the way my uncles hoped it would. Instead, it left me fearful and racked with guilt. But that psychological impact paled in comparison to the trauma one of my uncles inflicted at a different holiday gathering.

CHAPTER 5

CHRISTMAS SURPRISE

THROUGH MY SIX-YEAR-OLD EYES, Christmas morning was magical. A shiny, silver Christmas tree filled Grandma and Grandpa's large, arched front window. Two brightly colored bulbs at the base of the tree sent light flooding upward to reflect off the tree's hundreds of tiny silvery strips. The tree rotated slowly, creating a mesmerizing kaleidoscope effect.

Grandma and Grandpa were not rich, but on Christmas morning it felt like they were millionaires. An overflowing mound of presents spilled out from under the fake Christmas tree.

Once my aunts and uncles and cousins arrived, we packed into my grandparents' big living room. Grandpa began his methodical ritual of passing out the presents one by one. It always felt like it took forever for him to select each present and read the nametag before slowly handing the present to the appropriate person. As each gift emerged from its wrapping paper, everyone oohed and aahed.

Then, as typically happened every Christmas, midway through the mountain of presents, Grandpa tired of playing Santa and instead turned referee, blowing a whistle to signal it was time for the free-for-all. Everyone surged forward in a mad scramble to claim their remaining presents from under the tree and rip them open.

As usual, I stayed in the background, standing shyly on the outskirts of the wrapping-paper-shredding madhouse. Once the living room was strewn with a clutter of paper, bows, and discarded packaging and everyone had inspected their new toys, it was time to transition to all the food Grandma had prepared.

But just as Grandpa began to herd us from the living room into the kitchen, Uncle Dave—the war hero who was also a Golden Gloves boxer and judo champion—made a big announcement. "I have one more gift to give and wanted to save this one for last. It's for Greg," he said.

I was astounded. I was the misfit kid, not the favorite, the one whose manhood they were worried about.

I'd sensed for as long as I could remember that I didn't really belong in this brawny, brawling family. And they all sensed it too. They were worried about me. Sometimes, late at night, from up in my room, I overheard them talking about "toughening me up." They were afraid that not just the neighborhood but life itself would chew me up and spit me out.

All the adult family members gathered around the Christmas tree today—Ma, Grandpa, Grandma, and my aunts and uncles—weren't concerned about most of my other cousins.

Eric, David, Larry, Pam, Tammy, Jackie, and the rest of the crew were as tough as nails. They were scrappy. They knew how to handle themselves in a neighborhood where kids ran free and where might won out over right. Nobody bullied them.

But now on this Christmas morning, the most magical day of the entire year, despite my shortcomings, for whatever reason, Uncle Dave was giving me a special gift.

I stepped out from the shadows and joined the inner circle. Maybe this was my moment to shine. Maybe I did belong in this family after all.

Uncle Dave's beautifully wrapped present was passed from person to person to person as it made its way across the room toward me. My face was flushed with embarrassment, but my heart was full of pride. All eyes locked on me as I began to tear open the wrapping paper.

My heart was beating hard, not in anticipation of the gift so much, but because I had the attention of my entire family— maybe for the first time in my memory. I'd never felt so special.

But my heart dropped into my shoes when I saw what was inside. It was a baby doll, the kind of doll that came with a bottle and an extra set of baby clothes.

At first, I thought it was a mistake. I thought maybe he had got my gift mixed up with someone else's. Looking up at Uncle Dave across the room I said, "It's a doll."

The words he said next seared into my soul like a cattle brand. He looked right at me and said, "I figured since you don't have a dad, maybe you'd like to play with dolls like a little girl."

There it was. What others may have whispered to each other in back rooms, Uncle Dave said out loud in front of everyone. He summed up what many in my family thought of me. They were strong; I was weak. They were confident; I was cowering. They had powerful fathers; I had no father.

I had failed to live up to Grandpa's impossible standard of strength and Grandma's standard of toughness. My quietness was construed as wimpy weakness. I was right. I *didn't* fit into this rough, tough family.

And this was my reward—a girl's doll.

I erupted in unbridled rage.

Now my face was red for a whole other reason as I walked quickly and boldly across the room and shoved the doll into my uncle's stomach with a fury I didn't know I was capable of. "I AM NOT A GIRL!" I yelled.

The family roared with laughter at my unexpected, enraged response, but I saw a look of surprise flash across Uncle Dave's face. "Maybe he's one of us after all!" he observed.

I was confused. I didn't understand why the uncle I both idolized and feared would do something so cruel. And I had no clue why everyone was pleased about my angry reaction to the gift.

But the emotional trauma inflicted on me that day marked a new beginning. It triggered an awareness inside me that something was missing. And it launched me on a search for my true identity.

Even at age six, I could sense there was something more, a Presence who wanted to lead me out from the chaos to a place of safety, security, and significance. But at that age, I wasn't sure of the whys, the who, or the what. I just knew I had a big hole in my heart that was aching for more.

CHAPTER 6

"WELL, I AIN'T JESUS!"

I WASN'T THE ONLY ONE in my family trying to figure out my true identity. In the midst of this volatile, violent family, Uncle Jack was beginning to wrestle with how to live out his newfound identity in Christ.

The first thing I noticed after Jack got saved was his new obsession with the Bible, which suddenly appeared on the end table next to his favorite chair. I was surprised to see him reading it pretty much every time I was over at their house. But even more surprising was seeing him mark it up while he read it, underlining and highlighting things. I'd never seen anyone write in a book before—in fact, I thought it wasn't allowed—but Jack said it helped him understand and remember the things he was reading. Sometimes he would stop and tell Earlene about what he'd just read, and they would talk about it awhile. I didn't understand much about what they discussed, but sometimes things got a little heated, and they argued about what they thought it meant.

But even though Uncle Jack didn't always understand everything he read in the Bible, that didn't dampen his enthusiasm. He wanted to be strong in his faith, just like he was strong at the gym. He knew from working out that if you wanted to be the strongest guy in the room, then you needed to find the strongest guy in the gym and do exactly what he did. Jack figured that what was true of working out was true of studying the Bible. If you wanted to master the Bible, then it would be a smart move to follow the lead of someone who had already mastered it. So Yankee was his guy. Pastor Yankee Arnold marked up his Bible, underlining verses, highlighting passages, and jotting notes in the margin. So that's why Jack did the same thing when he read his Bible.

Jack and Earlene stopped sending Tammy and Jackie on the Sunday school bus and instead drove their whole family to church and Sunday school. Even in the middle of the week, the whole family would head off to church together to attend the Wednesday-night service.

Jack's sudden, radical conversion to Jesus not only astounded me and my family, it also sent shock waves across our neighborhood, leaving many wondering if his conversion was the real deal. Because Jack had quite a reputation.

At the meat-packing plant where Jack worked, his short, violent temper was legendary. Jack once told Grandma, Grandpa, and me the story of how he'd earned the respect of all his coworkers. One not-too-smart, humongous butcher who worked alongside him had developed a nasty habit of taunting him by cutting the strings of Jack's apron with his butcher's blade.

"Finally, I'd had enough," Jack explained. "'Cut my apron again, and I'll throw you headfirst into that vat of fat,' I told the guy, pointin' to the 55-gallon drum where we threw the fat from the carcasses we cleaned and cut.

"But the next day, the fool cut my apron strings again. So, without thinkin' or blinkin', I did my signature move on the guy's windpipe but with an added twist. I simultaneously grabbed his crotch hard, lifted him up over my head, and then threw him headfirst into the vat of blubber." Jack smiled at the memory.

"Then I calmly went back to work and left the guy headfirst and waist deep in cow fat. Eventually, another meat cutter ran up and kicked the vat over."

Jack paused for a moment for dramatic effect before adding, "And he never cut my apron strings again."

For obvious reasons, Jack was feared at the butcher shop by most and respected by all for his work ethic and his ability to military press a man twice his size over his head. Was it any wonder that some people were skeptical about his conversion to Christ?

Still, there was no denying that something dramatic had changed. Not only was he set ablaze by his passion for God, but he also became a spiritual arsonist, setting others on fire with the gospel too.

So he decided to start by talking to his coworker Thumper. Jack liked Thumper because he was a hard worker. Thumper was a bodybuilder too. He came from a large Catholic Italian family. And he was a straight shooter, which Jack respected.

Jack got the biggest kick out of telling anyone who would listen how God had arranged it all so that Thumper was ready to hear about the gospel before Jack even opened his mouth to try to bring Jesus up.

Thumper had come to work one day freaked out, which was out of character for him. He was one tough dude with substantial bodybuilding chops.

But he'd seen the movie *The Exorcist* over the weekend— the one about the girl who was demon-possessed. "That scene where her bed starts shaking really, really scared me," Thumper told Jack.

Jack knew this was his opening. "Well," he said, "I ain't afraid of the devil 'cause I have someone greater livin' inside of me—Jesus Christ!"

Thumper thought Jack was just joking, but he was dead serious.

Then Jack used the hand motions Yankee had shown him when he explained the gospel to Jack and Earlene. "I mighta messed it up some," Jack admitted to Thumper, "but here's the main message loud and clear—Jesus died for sinners, and salvation is a free gift to everyone who puts their faith in him. If you put yer faith in him, you become part of God's family forever. And, just like in a regular family, once yer in, nobody, not even the devil himself, can mess with you!"

Thumper had been a churchgoing Catholic all his life, but this was the first time Jesus' free gift of salvation really clicked with him. So he put his faith in Jesus right then and there in the butcher shop.

"You're no longer afraid of the devil, or death, or nothin', right?" Jack asked him, making sure Thumper understood the gospel of grace.

"Right!" Thumper said. "Now you gotta tell my whole family about this!"

"Hell, yeah!" Jack said.

For the next two weeks, Jack and Earlene went over to Thumper's house pretty much every day after work. There were eight people in Thumper's family—a good Catholic family— and all eight gathered around the dining room table most nights just to watch the fireworks between Thumper's mom, Dolores, and Jack.

First, Jack always told them about Jesus' free gift of salvation, and then Dolores always launched into him.

"Of course Jesus died for our sins," Dolores would say again and again, "but you still got to be good!"

So Jack always said back, "If we had to be good enough to make it into heaven, we'd all go to hell!"

Dolores would respond, "Not true. That's why we have confession and last rites and all those other sacraments!"

And all this time, Lonnie, the father of the family—who had been raised in a Baptist church—was sitting there, mostly quiet. But Jack could tell he was thinking hard about what Jack was saying, and so were all the rest of Thumper's brothers and sisters.

Again and again, night after night, Jack would read them the verses out of Ephesians that Yankee first told him about: "For by grace are ye saved through faith; and that not of yourselves: it is the gift of God: Not of works, lest any man should boast."

Finally, one night after Jack read those verses, he said, "If I buy you a gift on your birthday, I'm not gonna charge you for it.

It's a gift. So when the Bible says that salvation is a gift of God, it's a gift! Jesus paid for it with his own blood on the cross. You don't pay for it. You receive it!"

And over the next week, without telling their mom about it, one after another of the family had put their faith in Jesus.

"Winning a soul for Jesus is kinda like winning a fistfight, but even better!" Jack declared with a laugh when he told us the story.

Two weeks later Dolores gave in, too, and the whole family started going to Yankee's church with Jack.

That was another dramatic change I noticed in Jack: he was continually inviting people to come to church with him and Earlene. "Yankee gave the whole congregation a challenge," Jack explained. "Whoever brings the most people out to church over the next four weekends, Yankee's gonna give 'em a brand-new, leather-bound, King James Version, Old Scofield Reference Bible. Which is the exact same kinda Bible Yankee uses to preach from every week."

The King James Version was code for "no compromise" to Yankee. All other translations, according to his fundamentalist tradition, were weak at best and heresy at worst. To own and use an Old Scofield Reference Bible meant that the explanations for the passages on each page came from a dispensational theological point of view. It taught a pretribulational, premillennial, pre-everything view of the end times. Those who claimed to be fundamentalist (versus liberal) in their theology had better have the Bible backup to prove it. There was no better proof than wielding an Old Scofield Reference Bible—and the fact that it was both black and leather bound made it quite the treasure for Christians who were ultraconservative theologically.

"I'm gonna win it," Jack declared matter-of-factly.

For the next thirty days, Uncle Jack went on a redemption rampage. He invited his coworkers, fellow bodybuilders, weightlifters, tough guys, and street thug friends. Nobody liked saying no to Jack. And not many did.

Jack brought 250 guests to church in a single month. Of course, he was pleased that he won the Bible, but more importantly, he was thrilled that all of them had the opportunity to hear the gospel firsthand from the guy who had shared this message so boldly with him.

Although Jack had trusted in Jesus and was inviting pretty much everyone he knew to church, some of his old habits, especially when it came to violence, didn't change overnight. If someone he was sharing the gospel with wanted to argue or didn't accept the love of Jesus, there was a good chance he'd give them "the law of Moses" right upside their heads.

In the early '70s, long before big-box fitness centers littered the landscape like weights on a sloppy gym floor, the European Health Spa was one of the primo places to be. It boasted more than just the best barbells and weight machines on the market: it had steam rooms and saunas as well. It even had ice plunge pools to ease into after a hard workout to relieve your sore muscles.

Jack was proud of the fact that he had a lifetime membership at the European Health Spa, where he could press, curl, squat, and lift huge amounts of weight and impress other powerlifters and bodybuilders. He only weighed 185 pounds, but for his size, he was definitely the strongest man in the gym.

After his conversion to Christ, he still regularly went to the gym to strain for his gains with the best of them. Just because he was a follower of Christ was no excuse to be wimpy. But now, instead of just talking smack or shooting the breeze with his fellow bodybuilders, in between sets, he'd share the gospel with them.

At the gym, the size of his biceps was the only pass he needed to share Jesus with anyone and everyone. And, even if only for their own safety, they'd generally listen.

It was at that gym where one of his more infamous gospel-sharing stories took place. I first heard the story from Rico, the man he shared with, at a family gathering years later.

Jack and Rico had been sitting in the sauna after a hard workout at the gym when Jack started telling him about Jesus.

They were in a sauna, so they were buck naked, which was awkward to begin with, but Jack was determined to convert Rico regardless of the setting. "You're a sinner, just like me," Jack explained, "And you need to believe in Jesus, just like I did." Jack was just getting into it when things took a strange turn.

There was another guy in the sauna with them who had been sitting there quietly when he made the mistake of chiming in with his opinions about God and religion.

Jack turned to the guy and said, "Hey, I'm tryin' to tell this guy about the love of Jesus. Why don't you shut your mouth?"

Rico laughed when he told us the story. "Here was Jack talking about Jesus with me and threatening to go Old Testament on this guy!"

Determined, Jack kept sharing the gospel with Rico, but the guy interrupted again, trying to argue with him.

"If you interrupt me one more time, I'm takin' ya out!" Jack shouted.

Just as Jack turned back to Rico and started talking again,

the man interrupted again. Jack turned around, hit the guy with a short right hook on his jaw, and the man fell to the ground like a wet towel on the steam room floor.

The man pushed himself up from being flat on the floor, rubbed his jaw, looked up at Jack, and said, "Jesus didn't go around hitting people like that!"

"Well, I ain't Jesus. I'm Jack!" he replied.

There was no doubt that Jack was on fire for Jesus. When he'd said, "Hell, yeah!" to Jesus, he'd meant it. He carried himself with a new confidence, like he knew who he was and where he was going—even if there were some bumps along the road.

I, on the other hand, still had a big hole in my heart. I longed for a place of safety, security, and significance—like Uncle Jack seemed to have found. With Jesus in his life, he'd found new purpose at home, at work, at the gym, in the neighborhood—everywhere, really—while I still felt like a misfit in my family, a loser at my school, and a wimp in my neighborhood.

And things were about to get even more dangerous for me.

CHAPTER 7

AN ANGEL WITHOUT WINGS

"STOP RUNNING THROUGH THE HOUSE!" Grandma yelled.

Still running full speed, I turned my head toward her and yelled back, "Aww, Grandma, we're just having—"

But it was too late.

Crash!

I'd run straight into the door that led to Grandma's back porch, shattering the glass window that filled the top half of the door. My hands, which had been outstretched in front of me clenching a toy gun, had taken the brunt of the damage. My small body had hurtled halfway through the shattered window.

My legs hung on one side of the door's window frame while my chest, arms, and head dangled on the other side. Balancing like a teeter-totter between the inside and outside, I hung there in shock.

My brother, Doug, had been sitting on the porch when I came crashing through the window. "You're in big trouble," he said.

I knew instantly I was in trouble with Grandma. But I had no idea how right Doug was about being in *big* trouble—until I saw the blood.

My hands and wrists were pierced in what looked like a dozen places. Massive amounts of blood were gushing from a couple of the deepest cuts.

"Get some towels!" Grandma screamed at Doug. She'd turned pale and kind of greenish, like she might throw up.

I didn't cry. I just dangled from the window frame, balanced and bleeding until Doug and Grandma lifted me up and off.

Grabbing the white towels Doug had retrieved from the bathroom, Grandma tossed one back to Doug and barked, "Wrap that towel around that hand and wrist!" With shaking hands, Grandma wrapped a second white towel around my other gushing hand.

Once my hands and wrists were tightly wrapped, Grandma screamed further instructions to Doug. "Get all of the kids and take them out to the car! We've gotta go to the hospital!" Along with watching Doug and me while Ma worked, Grandma also provided childcare for other families. On summer weekdays, her house was typically full of kids scattered here, there, and everywhere. Thankfully, there were only two other kids with us that day.

Doug and Grandma corralled the other kids and crammed us three into the back seat of her light plum–colored 1959 Thunderbird. Then Doug climbed into the front passenger-side bucket seat.

The once-white towels wrapped around my hands and wrists were crimson red. I felt weak. I was losing blood fast. But Grandma was just sitting in the driver's seat. Her hands were shaking even more violently. She was terrified, and her fear terrified me. Never in my whole life had I seen Grandma scared, and now she was far beyond that point.

"Grandma, you better hurry," I said, woozy from blood loss but still not crying. Blood was dripping from the saturated towels onto the white leather interior. I was worried about getting in trouble for that, too.

But Grandma was worried about me. "God, help me!" she screamed. But still, we just sat there while Grandma grasped the car keys in her trembling hand, looking around her frantically.

Then, out of the blue, we heard three loud knocks on the car windshield.

Outside the rolled-up front passenger window, an elderly Black man was bent down, peering into the car with a look of concern on his face.

He was the first Black man I'd ever seen. Our part of North Denver was mostly Hispanic, with some Italian and a little bit of other, and the "other" didn't include many African Americans, since I'd reached the age of six and never seen a Black man in real life before.

"Are you okay, Ma'am?" he asked calmly. Somehow, his sincerity counteracted the distressing effect Grandma's panic was having on me.

"No!" Grandma screamed, reigniting my fear. "My grandson is bleeding out, and I'm so scared, I can't even find the keyhole to start my car!"

Taking command of the chaotic situation with an unusual

combination of gentleness and assertiveness, the man said, "Get out, ma'am. I'm driving you to the hospital."

Grandma opened the door, gladly shoved the keys into his hand, and told Doug to cram in the back with the rest of us. Then the man settled in behind the wheel and calmly drove us to St. Anthony Central Hospital.

"I'll wait here in the lobby with the other kids," the kind man told Grandma, "so you can stay with your grandson while they stitch him up."

After they wheeled me into the ER, they poked me in the arm with a big needle and pumped my blood-depleted body full of IV fluids and pain meds. Grandma was glued to my bedside, but she seemed calmer now, so I was too. I watched in fascination as they stitched my hands and wrists back together. It was bloody, but I had seen lots of blood before—just not my own.

After a few hours, the doctor released me, and the man drove us all back home.

"Goodbye," he said, after politely seeing us all to the door but never telling us his name.

"Thank you so much, sir! You saved my grandson's life," Grandma said with tears in her eyes.

Then he tipped his hat, smiled, and walked away.

For as long as I could remember, I'd feared for my safety. Tempers flared around me for no discernable reason. Violence erupted at the drop of a hat. But I'd always thought Grandma could protect me. Now I knew that even Grandma's house wasn't safe for me.

Still, who was that man who had appeared out of nowhere?

Had he been sent by Someone to help me—to save my life? And if so, why?

Years later, I stumbled onto a Bible verse that said, "Do not forget to show hospitality to strangers, for by so doing some people have shown hospitality to angels without knowing it."

Was the first Black man I ever met an actual angel or merely angelic?

I had no idea. But either way, I began to wonder whether Someone had sent him to save my life. If only I could figure out why and what it all meant.

Little did I know that only a few short months later, death would come knocking on my door again, leaving me even more confused and frightened.

CHAPTER 8

"COUNT BACKWARDS FROM TEN"

"QUICK, RUN AND HIDE," Grandma said, shooing me to safety when she saw my uncle Bob coming up the front steps. In a split second, I assessed the relative merits of running toward the kitchen to hide in the cabinet beneath the sink versus squeezing under my bed. Those were just two of the "safe" places where Grandma sent me to hide so my uncle couldn't torment me with threats that he was going to grind his cigar out on my arm.

I opted for the sink cabinet and took off for the kitchen in a mad dash. Crawling under the sink, I pulled the cabinet door closed behind me. In the darkness, I felt around for my trusty flashlight. When my searching fingers found their mark, I pushed the button, and light flooded my small space. Glancing around, my eyes fell on the picture book I'd been reading the last time I'd holed up here to escape the chaos around me. I heaved a sigh of relief. There was something calming about looking at the pictures and imagining myself in that storybook world—it looked safer and happier than the chaos that swirled around me every day. My book would be a welcome pastime while I was waiting for Grandma to give me the "all clear" that Uncle Bob had left.

Things could get ugly at my grandparents' big, red brick house during the brief intervals when one or the other of my uncles also temporarily moved in because they were running short of money and needed a fallback place to stay. Still, I preferred living at Grandma and Grandpa's house on Irving Street to living somewhere with just Ma and Doug and me. I knew Grandma loved me, and Grandpa was the only father figure I'd ever known. We'd moved around a lot up until we'd moved in with my grandparents. Moving from place to place was tough on an insecure, scared, and scarred kid like me.

So when Ma announced we were moving out of Grandma and Grandpa's house and into our own apartment over on Federal Boulevard, I was sad. I would miss being around my grandparents' house morning, noon, and night and playing in their yard on their relatively quiet street.

The apartment Ma, Doug, and I moved into was cramped, dingy, and noisy from the around-the-clock traffic floating up from the busy four-lane street below. It was also noisy because of the loud couple who lived upstairs. It sounded like they were doing construction projects day and night. Our flimsy, thin apartment ceiling did little to block out their banging, hammering, and stomping. We heard every bang and boom.

Not that Doug and I didn't contribute to the apartment building's noise level. It wasn't long before one of our favorite pastimes while Ma was at work was to blast out the siren-drenched song "D.O.A. (Dead on Arrival)" by Texas hard rock band Bloodrock. We would open all the windows in the apartment, and Doug would crank up the volume on the stereo as loud as it would go.

But the noisy dude who lived above us was even louder than we were, and he was one tough guy. He rode a Harley and was covered in scary-looking tattoos. One night after Ma got home from work, he was banging away particularly loudly on something. Ma had had enough. So she walked up the stairs and pounded on his door. When he opened it, he snarled out a nasty "Whaddya want?"

Ma sized him up, but he looked too big for even her to take—plus, she was tired after a long day on the job—so she tried a more diplomatic approach.

"Can you keep it down?" she asked him. "You guys are so loud, we can't hear ourselves think!"

The guy roared and cursed at her before slamming the door in her face.

She stood there for a few seconds considering the situation before coming back downstairs and calling Uncle Bob.

Within minutes, Bob arrived and pounded his big, angry fists on the Harley guy's apartment door. Bob and the guy yelled and cursed across each other for a while at the top of their lungs. Finally, the Harley guy shouted, "No way! I ain't apologizing!" Then he yelled back to his wife, "Get the gun!"

Not wanting to get shot right there at the guy's door, Bob grabbed him and threw him down the flight of stairs. Then he beat him to a pulp, while keeping one eye on the door at the top of the steps, making sure the man's pistol-packing wife didn't show up with guns blazing. "Now pack up and leave, or I'll give you worse if I ever lay eyes on you again!" Bob yelled as he retreated back to our apartment.

The amazing thing is that the Harley guy and his motorcycle mama did just that—they packed up and moved out the very next day.

And they were surprisingly quiet as they did.

But was that really the end of the story? Several months later, after Ma had moved us out of that apartment and on to the next place, we learned that the girl who moved into our old unit had been shot. Somebody had knocked on her door and when she put her eye to the peephole, she'd been shot clean through the door. Thankfully, she survived her gunshot wound. Still, Ma and I always wondered whether all those months later, the Harley guy had come back to our old place to wreak his revenge, and he'd shot the girl behind the peephole, assuming it was Ma.

Unfortunately, the Harley dude incident wasn't the only traumatic memory the apartment on Federal Boulevard held for Ma, Doug, and me.

"Something's wrong with Greg!" Doug screamed.

Rushing into my bedroom, Ma looked down at me, fear plainly written on her face. My scrawny body shivered uncontrollably as I convulsed in agony on my sweat-drenched sheets. Ma put a hand on my burning forehead.

"Oh no!" she screamed, before uttering a rare prayer. "God, don't let him die!"

Ma was at a loss. She had assumed I just had a fever when she had told me to go to bed early. I had been complaining about a pain in my tummy.

My small, trembling body was curled up into a tiny ball as

a result of the intense pain in my gut. Ma, grabbing my knees, which were pressed against my forehead, used all her might to try to uncurl me so she could get a better look and figure out what might be wrong with me.

But despite her barbaric strength, she couldn't pry me apart. Mom screamed, sensing something was horribly wrong with me. With a mother's instinct, she knew that if she didn't get me to the hospital ASAP, I was going to die.

Picking me up like a rag doll, she dashed out of the house, leaving Doug to fend for himself. After she laid me down in a ball on the passenger seat of her red Ford Pinto, we raced to St. Anthony Central—the same hospital where I'd almost bled out and died a few months before. A loud screech of the brakes announced our arrival at the ER. Carrying me under her arm like a football, she sprinted into the waiting room and screamed, "Get me a doctor *now*! My son is dying!"

Immediately, I was placed on a gurney and rushed into a room where a cluster of doctors and nurses worked to uncurl me. After assessing me, the doctor pushed back the large white curtain separating me from my ma and said, "Ma'am, we need to perform an emergency appendectomy."

"What does that mean? Speak in English!" Ma retorted sharply, half yelling and half crying, crazy with fear.

"His appendix has burst. Poison is coursing through his body. We have to remove the appendix right away and pump the poison out if we're going to be able to save him."

"Is he going to live?" Ma demanded.

"I hope so, but I don't know for sure," the doctor answered honestly. "An appendix that's been ruptured for a long time can lead to septic shock, which sometimes causes organ failure.

The bacteria and pus have spread like poison throughout his body."

Ma fell to her knees screaming and crying, "Oh God, no! Oh God, no! Oh God, no!" It was more of a shriek of desperation than a prayer.

Within minutes I was in the operating room, still racked with pain and scared to boot. There were people in white clothes and white masks all around me, lifting me from my rolling bed onto a hard table.

Where is Ma?

Soon, all the faces gathered around me and were looking down at my exposed belly. I heard a cool, quiet voice say, "Count backwards from ten."

I know how to do that. The thought that I could control something, even something as simple as counting backward, calmed me slightly.

"Ten . . . nine . . . eight . . . seven . . ." By the time I got to three, the room had faded to black.

I woke up staring at a white ceiling. I was in a strange bed in a strange room. Beeping noises surrounded me. *Where am I? Why is this plastic thing stuck up my nose? What's that noise? Where is everyone? Why do I hurt so bad?*

Vaguely the memory of doctors and nurses and writhing pain floated back to me. *This must be the hospital.*

Suddenly something somewhere behind my head kicked on with a loud motorized buzz. My innards felt like they were churning. Blackish-green gunk suddenly started oozing down the weird plastic straw that was stuck up my nose. *What's happening?* I was scared. And it hurt. A lot.

"Help!" I cried weakly.

Something stirred at the foot of my bed. I turned my head slightly to see what it was.

It was Ma! She was sitting in a chair she'd pulled up next to the foot of my bed. Her head and arms were stretched across the covers.

"Ma," I said hoarsely. Nothing. "Ma," I said louder. This time she heard me clearly and woke with a start.

"Greg, oh, Greg, you almost died!" she said. "I didn't know if you were ever going to wake up again. I've lived such a no-good, rotten bum of a life, I was afraid maybe God was gonna take you away from me."

For days, it had been touch and go for me. But something, or Someone, had finally touched my infection-ravaged body, and the grim reaper had been battled back and sent packing.

Why is death after me again? I wondered. *No other kid I know has almost died twice in a matter of months.*

This second battle shook my sense of security to the core. For as long as I could remember, my world had been a crazy, topsy-turvy, chaotic mess. My uncles were unpredictable. The neighborhood was full of gangs. I was bullied at school. The only two places I'd felt safe were at my grandparents' house and with my Ma—provided I stayed on her good side—which I was careful to do. Now, both of these safe havens had been ripped away. I'd almost died at Grandma's house, and now, under Ma's watch, I'd almost died again. Even Grandma and Ma couldn't fully protect me from whatever was stalking me.

Nowhere was safe.

CHAPTER 9

EARS BACK, TEETH BARED

MA HAD TO BE AT WORK EARLY each weekday morning, well before my school started, and since my brother wasn't driving yet, I was forced to make the long trek to and from school by myself.

Walking those ten blocks on school days filled me with an intense dread. There were all kinds of dangerous land mines along the way for a scared little third grader. It was like being in a scary movie where an imminent threat might be lurking around the next corner. I continually needed to be on high alert, ready to run or hide at the first whiff of danger as I walked my gauntlet of terror every school day.

The most obvious danger was the people. Ma had reconned the route with me, pointing out all the "bad houses" and warning me about who to avoid at all costs. Steering clear of the scary-looking people and bad houses like Ma told me to was one thing, but it wasn't just particular people living along my route that posed a risk. It was also the gangs.

Gangs were big in our neighborhood. You never knew when a car full of gang members—or wannabes—would pull up and try to mess with you. Plus, racial tension could spill over into a fight at any time, with or without gang affiliation. The Italians hated the Mexicans, and the Mexicans hated the Italians. Conflicts frequently erupted and often caused collateral damage.

But as scary as these gangs were to an eight-year-old kid walking to and from school, there was something else that scared me even more—two German shepherds, one big and one huge. These fierce dogs frequently escaped the confines of their poorly fenced backyard.

The owner was either unconcerned or clueless whenever the dogs escaped. They generally stayed in their own front yard while barking at anyone who wisely walked by on the other side of the street. Perhaps the owner figured that because the dogs had never crossed the street to attack anyone, there was nothing to worry about . . . until one fateful fall day.

It was a crisp October morning. Although the sun was shining, Denver's mile-high elevation had yielded, as usual, a dramatic temperature dip overnight into the thirties. As I packed up for the chilly walk to school, I pulled on my most prized possession—my black leather jacket. Just the leathery smell of it took me back to that memorable day when my dreams had come true and, uncharacteristically, Ma had bought it for me.

Every August before the new school year started, Ma would take my brother and me shopping at the Montgomery Ward bargain basement to buy school clothes. And that's when I'd seen it—a thick, slick, black leather jacket that looked just my size. And it was on sale!

Ma loved us boys, but she didn't like spending money she didn't have on things we didn't really need. I knew, even as an eight-year-old, that I would have to use all my powers of persuasion if I was going to have any shot at getting her to buy it for me.

"Hey, Ma, look at the great deal on this jacket!" I'd said.

Without even looking at the price tag, she'd shot back, "I'm not buying you a leather jacket, boy."

"But Ma, it looks pretty warm, and I need a new jacket anyway," I'd pleaded.

"What you need are two pairs of corduroy pants and two shirts, just like we get you every year," she'd responded.

But I was persistent. "Hey, Ma, my pants from last year still fit. What if we just got the jacket? It's leather, so it should last a long time, at least a few years. And it's 50 percent off! Please, Ma. Would you please buy me this jacket?"

She'd paused for a second and looked at the jacket, which was a good sign. But I knew the jacket would be mine when she inspected the price tag and said, "Well, that *is* a pretty good deal. Why don't you try it on so I can take a look at how it fits you?"

Once I'd put it on, it was as good as purchased, because Ma absolutely loved it. "It's a little big," she'd said, "but you'll grow into it. Let's get it!"

Even though we were bargain hunters and couldn't afford the finest, Ma took pride in the way we dressed. I'd walked out of the Montgomery Ward bargain basement with two pairs of corduroy pants, two shirts, and a really cool leather jacket.

So as I walked to school that chilly October morning, I

was toasty warm in black leather and relishing the fact that I looked just a bit like "the Fonz" from the sitcom *Happy Days*. Fonzie was the tough guy in the series who always dealt with the bullies and got all the girls. Even though I wasn't tough like the Fonz, I thought this jacket might make me look a bit more intimidating. As a small-framed white kid in the middle of the hood, I needed all the help I could get.

Little did Ma or I know her beyond-the-budget jacket purchase would likely save my life that morning when death came knocking for me a third time.

As usual, I was walking on the opposite side of the street from the German shepherd house, when out of the blue, the two dogs came charging across the street directly toward me, ears back, teeth bared. This took me totally by surprise because they weren't barking. But the look in their eyes was that of a predator, and the fear in mine made it clear that I was their prey.

Without thinking, I backed away from the sidewalk until I was up against the chain-link fence of the yard behind me. I covered my face with my crisscrossed arms and plunged my fingers into the diamond-shaped openings of the fence behind me. I closed my small fingers around the silvery metal webbing and held on with all my might, bracing for whatever was coming.

The dogs lunged full force into me, smashing me into the fence.

The bigger German shepherd locked his jaws around my tiny forearms, biting down hard as he pulled and twisted and tugged at me. The second dog lunged toward my abdomen, biting into the baggy part of my jacket. Thankfully, the fact that my jacket was a bit too large for me meant the dog got only a mouthful of jacket in his canine canines instead of my stomach.

Both dogs were using their full weight to alternately push me into the fence and tear me down from it. Every so often, one of them would release its bite in order to get a better grip on me. The bigger dog repositioned his bite again and again, determined to get a death grip on me and instinctively tried to shake me in his jaws like a dead rabbit. I could smell their dog breath and feel the saliva from the bigger dog as it dripped from his mouth down the leather sleeves and onto my face.

Even as an eight-year-old kid, I knew that if these dogs pulled me off the fence and got me to the ground, there was a good chance they would kill me. A third grader is no match for two full-size German shepherds in attack mode, and once my head and neck were no longer protected, I knew I'd be mincemeat.

With every bite, I let out a shriek. But I wasn't just screaming from the pain; I was shrieking in absolute terror, in fear for my life.

Seconds passed and nobody came to my rescue. I could feel my fingers starting to lose their grip. These two ferocious dogs were getting the best of me, so I screamed louder and louder and louder.

Just when my tiny white knuckles were about to give out, I caught a glimpse through my crossed arms of a figure hurriedly approaching. At first, I couldn't tell who it was, but a faint, female voice grew louder as the figure came closer.

It was Ma Zeemer, the wiry old woman who used to be our landlady at the little cracker-box house we lived at years earlier, at the time when Ma beat up my stepdad, Paul, with a baseball bat. Now, it was Ma Zeemer's turn to swing a bat like Babe Ruth.

She cursed and yelled at the dogs, "Get out of here!" There was a loud *crack!* One of the dogs let out a sharp, high-pitched squeal.

I don't know where Ma Zeemer learned how to swing that bat—maybe from watching Ma destroy Paul's car and beat him to a pulp—but she did a masterful job of hitting the dog without hitting me.

She cursed like a sailor and swung the bat again. With another loud *crack!* she landed a blow on the second German shepherd, hitting him square in the head. Both dogs, stunned by the blows, let go of me in seconds. But ominously, they didn't retreat. They just stood there on the sidewalk looking a bit dazed, trying to shake off the whacks to the skull they'd just taken. I was afraid they would attack again, so I stayed locked on the fence, retightening my grip.

But Ma Zeemer wasn't finished. She bravely jumped between me and the dogs, swinging her bat back and forth, yelling and screaming and cursing and calling down thunder on the devil dogs.

Apparently, the swinging bat and the screaming old lady were finally enough to spook the dogs. They tucked their tails between their legs and ran back to the safety of their own front yard.

I was badly shaken. Within minutes, the cops pulled up. "Let's check you out," one of the officers said to me. "Better take off your jacket so we can take a look."

Slowly, with hands still shaking from the adrenaline rush, I unzipped my battered jacket and slipped it off. My forearms were covered with what looked like chicken pox marks. "Well, I'll be," said the officer, shaking his head in amazement. "Look at those teeth marks all over his arms, and not a one of them broke through his skin." Then turning to speak directly to me, he added, "It's lucky for you that you were wearing that leather jacket."

It *was* lucky for me. You might even say it was providential. Because I was wearing that leather jacket, not one tooth of the bigger dog had pierced into flesh. And because my jacket was zipped up and a little bigger than it should have been, the German shepherds had only gotten leather and air in their jaws instead of my innards.

Over the next few years, I finally grew into that black leather jacket that had saved my life. I loved it even more than the day Ma bought it. In a sense, it was like soft armor that protected me from a very visible enemy.

Even as a kid, it seemed to me like this incident summed up how I felt about life. With each near-death encounter, I was growing increasingly fearful and insecure. It felt like something evil was after me. I could sense it in my spirit. I had no idea what "it" was, but I started to wonder if it wanted me dead.

I never saw those dogs again, and years later my grandma told me why.

"When your grandpa saw the bruises on your arms from the dog bites," Grandma explained later, "he was outraged. So he stuck the .357 in the back of his pants, walked down to the dog owner's house, and knocked on his front door. The guy opened the door and snarled, 'What do you want?'

"Your grandpa told him, 'I'm the grandfather of the kid your two dogs attacked today.'

"'The kid'll be fine. I heard the dogs didn't even bite through his jacket,' the guy told Grandpa dismissively, attempting to slam the door shut in his face.

"But your grandpa had stuck his foot in the door to keep it from closing. He pulled out his .357 magnum revolver and said, 'I just want to show you my gun. I have three bullets in it, two for your dogs and one for you if I ever see those dogs again, in your yard or out of it. If they're not gone by tonight, then I'll be back tomorrow and finish them and you."

The next day, the dogs were gone.

Once again, there had been danger. And violence. In my family, sometimes the violence was used to defend against the danger; sometimes it was used to attack. But the undercurrents of danger and violence were always there, waiting to erupt at unpredictable moments.

Yet so was love for God. The tension between these seemingly polar opposites confused me. Grandma and Grandpa went to church every Sunday, but they were renowned for their strength, toughness, threats, and, at times, extreme violence.

They were serious enough about their faith that a few years back, about the time Uncle Jack had trusted Christ, they had started taking my brother and me to church with them. Maybe they'd been shaken up, too, by my earlier near-death experiences. But I think they also felt bad that most of their kids had turned out pretty wild. Most all of their boys, plus my ma, had rebelled against their Baptist upbringing and embraced a life of extreme violence. Like a wet bar of soap, the harder Grandma and Grandpa had tried to squeeze their kids into religious conformity, the quicker they'd gone flying out of their grasp.

Perhaps Grandpa and Grandma saw Doug and me as their

second chance for redemption. Maybe if they took us to church every Sunday morning, they could get us headed down the right path. After all, they were older and wiser than when they had first started raising their own kids four decades earlier. We were their second shot at parenting.

So every Sunday they carted Doug and me to Bethany Baptist Church at 26th and Clay Street. Week after week, Grandpa would sing solos in church like "In the Garden" in his beautiful tenor voice. And like clockwork, Grandma would always fall asleep during the sermon but claim that she was "just resting her eyes."

My near-death experiences had spooked me and left me wondering about what happens after you die. And the traumatic doll incident on Christmas Day a few years back had stirred up questions in me about whether I was safe among my uncles and family and what I was designed to do. I was aimless, and the incident filled me with a longing for acceptance because I still hadn't found it in my immediate family. I felt like an outsider. So I wondered if maybe I might find some answers at Bethany Baptist.

Each Sunday, I listened intently to the preacher and my Sunday school teacher, but none of it made sense to me. At home, I scoured my little red Bible, often under the kitchen sink or behind the couch, but the Shakespearean King James language was hard to understand.

It was all so confusing. Mrs. Muirhead, my ancient Sunday school teacher, told us kids that if we wanted to escape the fires of hell, we needed to confess all our sins to God. That sent me into an OCD tailspin of perpetual, compulsive confession. I used my daily walk to and from school, when I wasn't running or hiding from bullies, to confess my transgressions. My internal conversations with God generally unfolded something like this:

Dear God, I confess my sin of anger toward my ma this morning. Oh yeah, and I confess that I didn't feel guilty about it at first. And I don't really feel guilty enough about it now. But I confess it.

Then I'd drop an f-bomb in my brain.

Dear God, I confess the f-bomb I just thought inside my head.

Over and over, the cycle would continue. Just when I thought I had confessed all my sins, I'd curse inside my head again. I was sure that if I died between the cursing and the confession, I would go straight to the lake of fire.

Once, I obsessed so much about going to hell, I literally peed my pants at the corner of 23rd and Irving—just fifty yards away from my grandparents' house—as I walked home from school.

I wasn't just confused; I was downright distraught.

Then one Sunday, Mrs. Muirhead abruptly changed her tactics. "Kids, if you want to go to heaven someday," she explained, "then you need to ask Jesus into your heart today."

I knew from Uncle Jack's story that knowing you would go to heaven was a big deal. I knew from my near-death experiences that death could catch up with me anytime. But I had no idea what asking Jesus into my heart meant. To me, the heart was a literal, beating organ of your body. But dutifully, I tried to ask Jesus to come in there. My daily prayers took an anatomical twist: *Dear Jesus, come into my heart.* Then I'd pause to see if anything felt different. *Are you there?* Again, I'd pause and wait to see if anything felt different inside my chest cavity. *If you are in my heart, please say something or nudge something. Knock three times if you're there.*

Once again, my constant attempts at a "salvation" experience weren't working out for me.

I was fearful that if I coughed too hard, I'd dislodge Jesus from my heart. I imagined that if I ever needed a heart transplant, then I'd be headed straight to hell, because, well, there goes Jesus!

All of this further scared, scarred, and confused me.

My home life was a mess. I had never met my biological father. I was afraid of my own family. My neighborhood was scary, and I'd almost died three times in two years. Nowhere was safe or secure. Now, on top of all that, I realized that if I were to die in my current condition, I'd be going straight to hell. That sixth sense I'd had since the dog attack that "something" was after me intensified.

Then one Sunday, everything changed.

CHAPTER 10

FLIPPING OFF THE DEVIL

I REMEMBER IT like it was yesterday.

Grandpa sang a beautiful solo during the church service that morning. Pastor Claude Pettit preached his sermon. And Grandma rested her eyes.

In closing, Pastor Pettit said, "If there's anyone here today who would like to get saved, join the church, or be water baptized, just walk the aisle while the music plays and tell me what you've decided. Don't be ashamed. Come down the aisle today."

I'd repeatedly confessed every possible sin and countless mental curse words. I'd asked Jesus into my heart a thousand times and recited endless versions of the sinner's prayer. *Why not get water baptized?* I thought. *Maybe that will help.*

So, tugging on my Grandpa's sleeve, I whispered, "Grandpa,

I'd like to be water baptized. Would you go down the aisle with me?"

He smiled and nodded, and together we stood up and made our way out of the pew. As the organist played "Just as I Am," I walked the center aisle hand in hand with my grandpa.

Pastor Pettit leaned down to me and asked, "Why did you walk the aisle today, son?"

"I want to get water baptized," I said simply, gazing up at his towering figure.

And then he said the words that changed everything. "Before you get water baptized, you must be a Christian. That means that you believe that Jesus died on the cross in your place for your sins and that you've put your faith in Jesus to forgive you for your sins and give you everlasting life. Have you done that?"

In that moment, time stood still, because the message of the gospel made sense to me for the very first time. At last I had clearly heard how my sins could be forgiven. It wasn't by confessing all my sins, or asking Jesus into my heart, or saying the magic words of some sinner's prayer. It was by putting my faith in Jesus and what he had done for me on the cross.

It finally all made sense.

"Son," Pastor Pettit asked again, snapping me out of my epiphany, "have you put your faith in Jesus?"

Right then, in the quietness of my soul I prayed my own, genuine, heartfelt sinner's prayer. *Jesus, I believe you died and rose again. I trust in you to forgive me for all my sins and to give me eternal life!*

"Yes!" I declared to Pastor Pettit. "I've put my faith in Jesus!"

With that, Pastor Pettit announced to the church my "willingness to submit to believer's baptism." The congregation responded with light applause and a smattering of hearty Baptist amens.

Pastor Pettit invited me to stay at the front so that the congregation could congratulate me on my decision to get baptized. As I shook hand after hand, I marveled at what had just happened. *These people have no idea that I just now put my faith in Jesus.*

I felt like the weight of Mount Everest had been lifted off my shoulders and cast into the deepest sea. It felt like I was floating on air. At last I knew that all my sins were forgiven! I knew that, beyond my crazy family situation, there was something bigger, there was *Someone* bigger, and that Someone had given his life for me because he loved me! And I knew that even if I died, I'd be safe and secure in heaven with Jesus!

After church we piled into Grandpa's yellow Ford F-150 truck with the camper shell on back. On the drive home I told Grandma how excited I was that at last I believed!

Grandma lifted my little red Bible from my hands and penned these words in the front: "Greg Stier received Jesus Christ as his Savior on June 23, 1974." All these years later, I still have that Bible. I cherish it and the memory of that momentous day that changed my life for all eternity.

The next week in Sunday school, I boldly rebuked Mrs. Muirhead for not clearly explaining the gospel to us kids. "All this 'confess your sins' and 'let Jesus into your heart' stuff doesn't make sense to us kids," I scolded. "You need to tell people about what Jesus did on the cross!"

She was speechless because I was only eight years old at the time.

But now, things were starting to click. I knew that I actually *did* have God in my heart, finally. And, after the dog attack, I had sensed that I had an enemy, too. Now I realized my enemy was the devil.

Across the following months, as I began to learn more about God from the Bible, I also wanted to learn more about my enemy. I asked my grandparents and my Sunday school teachers about the devil and his demons. What were they up to? How did they operate?

I scoured the Scriptures and discovered 1 Peter 5:8: "Be alert and of sober mind. Your enemy the devil prowls around like a roaring lion looking for someone to devour." The image of a roaring lion reminded me of those two vicious dogs that had attacked me. Just like those dogs, it became clear to me that Satan and his demons wanted to drag me down and kill me.

I read John 10:10, where Jesus says, "The thief comes only to steal and kill and destroy; I have come that they may have life, and have it to the full." Even though Satan wanted to steal my identity, kill my hopes, and destroy my future, Jesus wanted to give me life—true life, full life.

I was keenly aware of both God and the devil. And in my underdeveloped, preadolescent brain, it made perfect sense to me that if I was commanded to love God, then the opposite was also true: I should hate the devil.

So I hated him with a vengeance. I whispered threats under my breath to him as I walked to school. *Someday I'm going to do great things for God just to tick you off. I hate you, Satan.* All I knew was that I wanted to taunt Satan for the rest of my life by living for God full bore.

In my young mind I imagined that hell and Satan resided somewhere in physical space down beneath the ground. So one day, while I was walking down the hallway of Brown Elementary School, I pointed both of my middle fingers straight down toward the floor. In my mind, I was perfectly justified giving the devil "the bird." He'd been attacking me and my family for years, so I wanted him to know that I wasn't happy about it. One of the teachers stopped me and asked, "What are you doing with your middle fingers?"

Irritated that he'd interrupted me, I replied curtly, "What do you think I'm doing? I'm flipping off the devil!"

Stunned, the teacher just stood there speechless as I walked away, still displaying my absolute contempt for the devil and his demon dogs running amok.

In a way, I've been flipping him off ever since.

CHAPTER 11

THE KILL SWITCH

"HOW ABOUT SOME MORE?" Uncle Bob asked his friend Mike, the owner of the bar.

"Sure! Let me pour you another!" Mike said, filling Bob's six-ounce glass with a megashot.

At 104 proof, peppermint schnapps was quickly getting Bob drunk, which was the point of this particular gathering. Their buddy, Doug Johnson, held up his glass for a refill too. Doug was a hard-drinking, fast-living fighter. He and Bob came from the same North Denver neighborhood and had known each other since they were kids.

It was late on a Sunday afternoon at the Silver Dollar Bar and Grill, hailed as one of the toughest bars in Denver. In Colorado in the '70s, state law required that bars stay closed on Sundays, so Mike, Bob, and Doug had the place to themselves.

Bob worked there on Friday and Saturday nights as a bouncer for Mike. He didn't work for money but for free drinks and for the sheer enjoyment of the fights that often broke out.

Uncle Bob was born to be a bouncer. He scared me to death. He was no bodybuilder, but he was as strong as an ox. At his day job as a pipefitter for the railroad, he was renowned for being able to move 500-pound pipes single-handedly. No one else at his company came close to his level of power. He wasn't a man to be trifled with. Like Grandpa, he never worked out but was naturally, freakishly strong.

Being from North Denver and the youngest of five fighting brothers and one fighting sister, Bob had honed his bare-knuckle fighting skills in countless living room brawls with siblings and frequent back-alley fights with gang members.

My earliest memories of Uncle Bob were terrifying. When he'd see me, he'd say, "Come over here, you little—!" And then he'd reach out to try to grab me as I ran away and hid. What he probably meant as playful chiding, I took as a horrifying, imminent threat.

The violent stories he told again and again were like oxygen to him. He breathed them in and exhaled them out to anyone who would listen.

I don't remember when I first heard the story about this particular night at the Silver Dollar from Uncle Bob, but it was the *one* fistfight story that had a different ending for Bob—and for our family.

Mike and Doug loved Uncle Bob. He was loyal, fun, and always had your back, especially in a fistfight. As the three buddies sat at the bar downing repeated supershots of peppermint schnapps, Bob and Doug were leaning on Mike to

With my brother, Doug,
in the backyard of my
grandparents' house. Not
long after this someone
poisoned our dog.

A kiss for Ma at my
high school graduation.
My buddy Rick Long is
in the background.

My brother and I have been close
through thick and thin.

I don't remember the drums or the
hat, and I don't take responsibility
for my lack of proper attire.

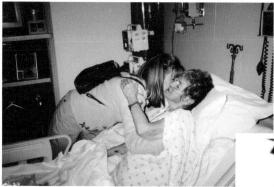

My wife
hugging Ma
in hospice.

*Uncle Dave flying his rescue chopper in Vietnam.
He received over 40 medals and commendations!*

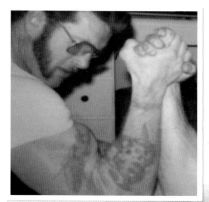

*Uncle Jack arm wrestling another
bodybuilder. He only weighs 185 lbs.
in this picture!*

*The family God
has blessed me
with ... Debbie, my
amazing wife, and
Jeremy and Kailey,
our great kids!*

join them on their next escapade. "Mike, I'm tellin' ya," Bob said enthusiastically, "we'll get twelve cases of beer, whiskey, vodka, the works, and we'll spend ten days in the backwoods outside of Granby. I know this great camping spot just outside Rocky Mountain National Park."

"I'm not lugging that much stuff into some backwoods campsite," Mike said, interrupting Bob's sales pitch.

"Didn't we tell you?" Doug said, jumping in. "We're gonna rent pack horses! We'll load 'em up and ride 'em in. You won't have to lug a thing! It's gonna be real Wild West!"

"Fishin', campin', shootin', drinkin', drinkin', and more drinkin'," Bob added, triggering a big group laugh.

"Sounds like fun. But I'm just too busy with the bar," Mike explained. But Doug and Bob went to the same school of persistence and insistence.

"You need to come hang with the boys!" Bob continued, cursing and pounding the table as he slammed down his empty shot glass.

"I don't know," Mike muttered. "I'll think about it."

The three were already intoxicated as the late afternoon turned to evening. Especially Doug.

"I gotta get home," Bob said, glancing at his watch. "Can you give me a ride, Doug?"

"Sure thing!" Doug said enthusiastically, oblivious to the fact that he was drunk as a skunk.

"I'll walk you guys out," Mike volunteered.

Unsteadily, the three friends made their way to the parking lot, where Doug's brand-new yellow convertible Porsche 914 was parked diagonally across two spaces.

"Why'd you park like that, Doug?" Mike asked.

"I don't want anyone scratching my baby," Doug explained, gently patting the hood of his car.

Bob's large, muscular frame plopped down into the tiny passenger seat of the small, sleek, fast sports car. With the weight of his frame, the car chassis sank a couple inches closer to the ground. Bob was one big boy. He looked like an offensive lineman sitting in a go-kart. His head jutted above the windshield, his knees were crammed against the dashboard, and his frame spilled over the center console.

Once Doug climbed into the driver's seat and rolled down his window, Mike squatted down, resting his forearms on the driver's side of the Porsche to continue the conversation. Doug was still trying to talk Mike into joining them on the upcoming camping trip.

Doug was so focused on his drunken dialogue with Mike that he somehow failed to notice the drug-crazed man who had jumped onto the hood of the Porsche and was standing on it ranting incoherent threats to no one in particular.

"What are you doin'?" Bob yelled. "Get off the car!"

Still clueless, Doug turned to Bob and asked, "Why are you screaming?"

Bob pointed to the man who was now bouncing up and down on the car hood and incredulously asked Doug, "You gonna let this guy jump on your car like that?"

"Get off my car!" Doug screamed.

Bob's street smarts kicked in, and he opened his door to get out, assuming the inevitable. As anticipated, the maniac jumped off the hood in Bob's direction and took a swing at him.

Big mistake.

Bob threw the man up against the building and threatened

him. "Get out of here, or I'm going to break you in two!" Thinking the incident was over, Bob pushed the guy away and headed back toward the car.

"Not so fast!" Doug yelled, lunging full speed toward the guy who had desecrated his prized possession with boot marks.

In a flash, Doug tackled the stark-raving-mad man. Curse words flew like fists as they went at it on the ground. Bob and Mike, like trainers during a boxing match, barked out advice to Doug.

"Get on top of him and pummel his face!" Bob yelled.

"Headbutt him!" Mike urged. "What are you waiting for?"

In the evening shadows of the building, it was hard for Bob and Mike to clearly see what was happening. But once they caught sight of the blood, they realized this was not a typical brawl.

The enraged, psychotic man had pulled out a knife with a five-inch blade and was slashing away at Doug as they rolled around on the ground. The parking lot wrestling match had turned into a bloodbath.

Mike got to the pair first, with Bob close behind. In a flash, the perpetrator scrambled to his feet and stabbed Mike in the gut. Then wheeling around, he set his sights on Bob.

Bob, who knew plenty about street fighting, instinctively realized that he needed to get a little distance between him and his knife-wielding attacker so he could get his bearings and figure out how to get the knife away from him without getting stabbed himself. Even in his drunken stupor, Bob knew if he could somehow draw the man away from his two bleeding friends, then maybe he could keep the guy from stabbing them again.

So as the man came at him, Bob swept his legs out from underneath him. But when the crazed man immediately jumped back up, Bob turned and ran, trying to draw the guy away from his friends. After a few seconds, he checked behind him to make sure the man had taken the bait and was chasing after him.

He wasn't.

But thankfully, he wasn't attacking Doug and Mike, who were moaning on the ground from their stab wounds. Instead, Bob caught sight of the man as he disappeared around the back corner of the bar. Never one to let a perpetrator escape, Bob followed in hot pursuit.

Rounding the corner of the building at full throttle, Bob was surprised to see the crazed man cowering against the graffiti-covered back wall of the brick building. Bob kept running, his large frame picking up momentum with every step. Like an unstoppable freight train, he ran straight at the guy, hoping to get to him before he realized what was going on. Cocking back his long, strong right arm, he swung it like a catapult toward the man's head. Bob's giant fist hit the guy so hard that his head bounced off the brick wall like a rubber ball before hitting the concrete curb below.

But Bob didn't stop there. With a mixture of adrenaline, terror, and alcohol surging in his veins, he kept punching and punching. Bob was terrified that this guy still had the knife. And he was horrified that two of his best friends might be dead from their stab wounds.

With every punch to the guy's face, his skull would fling back with a jolt. But Bob kept dropping his fists on him like a sledgehammer until everything was drenched blood-red—the man's face, his shirt, the curb, Bob's hands, his clothes, and his boots—everything.

The kill switch had been flipped.

It was the kill switch that made my family so dangerous. When most men get in a fight, there's posturing and threats first. Words are exchanged, eyes are narrowed, voices are raised, and chests are puffed. Before things ever escalate to throwing punches, there's usually some sort of pushing match first.

But not in my family. When the switch was flipped, my family acted. Like a muscle car that can go from 0 to 60 in 3.5 seconds, my family got to unbridled rage in no time flat. When the kill switch flipped, only one thing was in view: the utter and absolute destruction of their enemy.

No one really knows how long it was before the cops arrived, but by the time they showed up, lights flashing and sirens blaring, the guy was gone—his eyes had rolled into the back of his head.

One of the cops who knew Bob from the old neighborhood rushed him and tried to throw a choke hold on him. But Bob's explosive rage instantly shifted from the perp to the police, so he turned on the cop and slammed him onto the hood of his own squad car.

Then all the cops rushed Bob at once and got him to the ground. After handcuffing him, they took off his blood-covered boots, perhaps as evidence, or perhaps to slow him down if he tried to escape. Then they threw him into the back of the squad car, slammed the door, and left him there. An ambulance pulled up, and two EMTs jumped out.

From where he sat in the back of the squad car, Bob watched the EMTs doing chest compressions on the man in a desperate—and futile—effort to get his heart kick-started again. They finally put him on a gurney and wheeled him to the ambulance as fast as they could.

A cop came back and opened the squad car door. "He's dead. You'll be charged with manslaughter," the cop told Bob before reading him his rights.

"In that moment," Bob told my family later, "I started weeping uncontrollably. I wept for the man I'd just killed. I wept for my friends who might die of their stab wounds. And I wept for my own life, which would soon be lived out behind bars.

"But it was there in the back of the cop car," Bob explained, "where I called out to God for the first time since I was nine years old. Way back then, I'd put my faith in Christ after hearing a sermon on hell in church. Then in my teen years, I drifted from God and got caught up in the violence and partying all around me. Now, here I was in my twenties, and my life was a big fat mess. I figured I was probably headed to jail for a good part of my life for killing some guy."

But even though Bob had drifted from God, God had not drifted from him. God was right there in the back of the squad car with Bob the whole time—waiting, longing, and never giving up on his wayward son.

Faced with the stark reality of what had just happened, Bob called out to God, "God, forgive me! Help me! Rescue me! I'll serve you for the rest of my life with everything I got."

Humbled and broken, Bob spent the night in jail. "There, in the midst of the other felons, I didn't sleep a wink," Bob recounted. "I prayed for my friends who had been stabbed, hoping they'd somehow survived. And I trusted my future to God, no matter how bleak. I thought through the life I'd wasted and wondered what would happen next. The one thing I did know was that, in jail or out of jail, I was all-in to serve God for the rest of my life."

And when my family says they're all-in, they're all-in.

Around noon the next day, a police officer came to Bob's jail cell. "Come with me," he said curtly. Then he escorted Bob up to the fifth floor of the building and handed him off to a detective.

"The guy you beat up last night was fully resuscitated," the detective said.

"What?" Bob asked in disbelief. "He's still alive? Last night, the cop said I killed him!"

"Yeah, that's what we thought at the scene," the detective explained, "but the EMTs got his heart beating again in the ambulance. At the hospital, the doctors discovered the knife hidden on him that was covered with your friends' blood."

"Are they okay?" Bob asked.

"Both of them are gonna survive too and should be out of the hospital soon," the detective said. "But that guy you almost beat to death will be in recovery for a long time. We were already looking for him 'cause he stabbed a cop earlier. The guy's a nut job."

"So what about me?" Bob asked.

"We're dropping the charge of manslaughter and releasing you," the detective said nonchalantly, not even bothering to look up from his paperwork.

"I was stunned," Bob told us later. "I walked out of that building a free man in every sense of the word."

And true to his word, Bob started living for God. It had been years since he had been in a church. But one thing was for sure: he didn't want to go back to his parents' old Baptist church full of blue hair, walkers, and the smell of Mentholatum ointment. Bob remembered Uncle Tommy and Aunt Carol telling him, "There's lots of pretty girls at Yankee's church. You should check it out." And once he did, it was game over. Bob found where he was supposed to be.

It wasn't just the pretty girls, the worship, the building, or even Yankee that impressed him. Yankee told corny jokes and preached long sermons. What captured Bob was the simplicity of the message and the urgency of the mission. Yankee made things crystal clear, especially the message of salvation. He'd use his hillbilly charm and simple but effective visual illustrations to break things down so that they came alive in a way Bob could understand and apply to his life.

But most significantly, Yankee helped Bob understand that he had an important job to do—that he was needed. Up until then, Bob's only job was pipefitting and throwing drunks out of the bar. But Yankee repeatedly prodded him, asking, "Everyone can do something to reach someone with the gospel. What are you going to do, Bob?"

Bob's initial response was blunt—he had no idea.

But Yankee had an idea.

CHAPTER 12

WHAT ABOUT BOB?

YANKEE HAD A STRANGE VISION for Bob. He envisioned Bob as a captain in the church's bus ministry for Sunday school.

Could the same man who possessed a hair-trigger kill switch drive a bus full of kids to church? It was hard to believe it could be true. But it was. Even I wasn't afraid of Bob anymore. He'd been transformed from a raging grizzly bear to a teddy bear, almost overnight. Only God could have transformed Bob from a street fighter to an evangelist to children across the city!

Back in the '60s and '70s, bus ministries gained popularity through the leadership of Dr. Jack Hyles, the controversial pastor of the First Baptist Church of Hammond, Indiana. Hyles had built the largest Sunday school ministry in the nation by deploying school buses all over Hammond and the surrounding areas—including the city of Chicago—to pick up children and bring them to his Sunday school. Every week, thousands of children were bused in to hear about Jesus.

He and his team of bus captains were so effective at reaching young ones for Christ that Hyles started doing conferences to train other church leaders. Thousands of pastors and church leaders from across the nation attended his conferences to learn from his efforts.

Yankee was just getting his bus ministry started and was planning on taking a group of potential bus captains to attend the next Hyles conference. He invited Bob to be part of the group that was driving from Colorado to Indiana to see firsthand what a successful bus ministry looked like. Bob agreed to go. After hearing Dr. Hyles rant and rave about the need for reaching children with the gospel, Bob signed on to be one of Yankee's bus captains so more children could hear about Jesus.

But Bob wasn't content just to have a bus route that picked up kids every Sunday morning. He wanted to have the biggest bus route in Yankee's ministry. He told Yankee that his goal was to break one hundred kids on one bus (even though the maximum official capacity was seventy-two!).

Bob threw himself into the bus ministry the way he used to throw himself into fights—full bore, giving it his all. Every Saturday morning, he'd drive to apartment complexes and trailer courts loaded with candy and popcorn and prizes to hand out to kids. He'd go to the poorest parts of the city and go door-to-door, introducing himself to parents, telling them his story, sharing the gospel, and encouraging them to let their kids ride the church bus to Sunday school the next day.

Parents putting their kids on a bus with a total stranger is unthinkable today, but a generation ago, it was a weekly occurrence in many cities and towns across the country. "Get 'em saved young" was the mantra, making bus ministries a big outreach focus in many Baptist and conservative churches at the time. And it worked! God used bus ministries to reach tens of thousands of children for Christ all over the United States.

As a result of Bob's open, authentic, sincere love for Jesus, many moms and dads were comfortable letting their kids go with him to church. And the kids absolutely loved him.

When I was ten years old, Uncle Bob let me tag along on his bus. He had recruited my uncle Jack to be the bus driver on his pickup route. It shocked me to see these two men who had once tormented and terrified me laughing and joking with all the kids. Uncle Bob, who just a few months earlier had been in jail for manslaughter, ran up and down the school bus aisles, roaring with laughter as he kidded around and played games with them.

As the bus made its rounds, we sang praise songs to Jesus at the top of our lungs.

Could this be the same man I used to hide from at Grandma and Grandpa's house? The truth is, he was *not* the same man; in fact, neither of them were the same men they used to be. I could see that with my own eyes. Their faces shone with joy, where once I saw only furrowed brows and dark, angry eyes.

If these other kids only knew . . . , I thought to myself. If they could have seen Bob and Jack the way they used to be, they would have been terrified. They would be running away instead of laughing and joking.

But Bob and Jack had been made new in Christ. The kill switch had been replaced with a new switch—reaching kids with the gospel.

Once Bob finally achieved his one-hundred-rider goal for his Sunday school bus route, he decided it was time for his next big challenge. "I'm going to Florida Bible College," he announced at a big family dinner one Sunday at my grand-parents' house. I was shocked. Bob was a Colorado boy through and through. He loved to hunt in the mountains and fish in the rivers and drive the city streets of Denver.

I wondered what a Bible college was, anyway. Whatever it was, it had the word "Bible" in it, so I thought it must be a good thing.

While this news totally surprised our family, it absolutely astounded his old drinking buddies and street-fighting friends, who thought Bob had gone Jesus crazy.

True to his word, Bob packed up his stuff and moved to Florida Bible College (FBC) at the end of the summer. Although he was twenty-six years old, he felt like a kid again, absorbing God's Word in his classes and deepening his relationship with God while holding firm to his passion for telling others about Jesus.

But learning how to walk with Jesus can be a sticky, messy process. Just like with Uncle Jack, Bob found that his kill switch sometimes switched back on even after his come-to-Jesus moment.

Soon after he started attending the college, Bob met the girl who would one day become his wife, a tall, big-smiled beauty from South Carolina named Diane. One Saturday night after a late date with Diane, Bob sneaked back into his dorm room, being careful not to wake up his roommate, Tony.

The next morning was church, which was held downstairs, right there in the dorm. But instead of getting up to go to church, Bob slept in. Besides the fact that he'd gotten in late on Saturday night, he was exhausted from school, studies, and his work as a plumber for the school.

That's when Jerry, a fellow student at the college, barged into Bob's room to wake him. During the church service, Jerry had been thinking about something that he was convinced God wanted him to talk to Bob about. So, dressed in his white dress shirt and oversize 1970s necktie, Jerry walked out of church and marched up the stairs, down the hallway, and into Bob's dorm room.

"Bob, get up! I need to talk to you!" Jerry said urgently.

"What's going on?" Bob asked, cursing, groggy from being roused out of a deep sleep.

"Don't curse at me!" Jerry replied piously. "The Lord frowns on it. Just like he frowns on you locking your dorm room door at night. I should be able to come into your room anytime to fellowship with you and Tony. Get up right now, Bob. The Lord wants us to talk."

Jerry was a legalistic guy who held on to rules the way dogs hold on to ham bones. And like a dog, he wouldn't let this go.

"Get out of here! I'm trying to sleep," Bob yelled at him, cursing again, raising the intensity of his voice to scare this modern-day Pharisee away.

It didn't work.

"I'm not leaving. The rules state clearly that room doors should not be locked, and you lock your door all the time. We are going to straighten this out right now," Jerry insisted.

The kill switch was about to flip. Bob growled from underneath the covers. "If you don't get out of here right now, I'm going to beat the s— right out of you!"

Naively underestimating Bob's capacity for violent rage, Jerry stood his ground. "I don't care what you do to me," he said. "I'm *not* leaving until we figure this out."

With that, Bob sprang out of bed, his huge frame clothed in nothing but tighty-whities. In a flash, he picked Jerry up off the ground and slammed him full force onto the dorm room floor.

Realizing that he had literally awakened a sleeping giant, Jerry scrambled to get up and ran for the door, but Bob grabbed him by the back of his shirt with one hand and hammered the side of his head with blows from the other.

"Jesus, help me!" Jerry screamed, trying to escape from Bob's vise grip on his shirt.

But as he pulled away, Bob's grip on the back of his shirt was so tight that all the buttons in front popped off and Jerry's shirt was completely ripped off him. Shirtless, but still wearing his oversize tie, Jerry ran for the door and down the hallway, screaming, "I'm gonna tell the president of the college what you did to me!"

Bob ran after Jerry and tackled him in the hallway. "You ain't tellin' nobody nothin'!" Bob yelled.

Grabbing Jerry by his necktie, Bob dragged him back to his dorm room, threw him in, and locked the door behind them.

"You wanna talk," Bob said, "let's talk."

By the time Bob's roommate, Tony, came back to their dorm room after church, Jerry was in tears. Tony, shocked at the sight of his bleeding, shirtless next-door neighbor—who frequently barged into their room day and night without being invited—and his underwear-clad roommate, asked, "What the heck is going on?"

Between sobs, Jerry whimpered, "I was wrong. I shouldn't

have been judging Bob for locking the dorm room door. I shouldn't have woken him up from a dead sleep." Jerry was apologizing profusely for anything and everything in a desperate effort to keep Bob from flying into another rage.

Bob just sat there quiet, disappointed that all it took was a loud voice early in the morning to flip that dreaded kill switch. Like Grandpa and Jack before him, Bob was realizing that while being saved from the penalty of sin happened instantly at the moment of salvation, being saved from the power of sin is a lifelong struggle.

FBC was a great place for Bob to learn how to live for Jesus and better fight his battle with sin. Yankee had graduated from FBC less than ten years earlier. It was the epicenter of the gospel movement that had given Yankee his crystal-clear gospel messaging and his crystal-clear vision for reaching young people for Jesus.

From the start, FBC's emphasis was youth ministry. Its legendary founder, Dr. A. Ray Stanford, had been saved later in life. Shortly after his conversion, he had started a youth ministry in his own home that ballooned to a couple hundred teenagers. As his ministry grew, he spawned other youth ministries and nicknamed them "Christian Youth Ranches." Although "Christian Youth Ranch" sounded like a reform school run by priests for wayward kids, teenagers came out in droves.

Ray believed that teenagers came to Christ quicker and spread the gospel faster than adults, so even though he eventually planted a church, deep down, he really viewed his church as a means to fund and fuel his youth ministry.

As his youth movement grew, thousands of teenagers from all across South Florida began attending Youth Ranches. Once teens got saved, they were trained to grow and go. From square one, they were equipped to share the gospel and unleashed to do it. The result was teens reaching teens, who, in turn, reached and discipled even more teens.

What Jack Hyles was to Sunday school bus ministry, Ray Stanford was to youth ministry. Because of his driving passion for reaching and discipling young people, Ray launched Florida Bible College, which helped propel the Youth Ranch movement beyond South Florida. By the mid-70s, the college had well over a thousand students, many of whom had been reached by the Christian Youth Ranches across the United States—including the one Yankee had started in Arvada, Colorado.

Yankee's Youth Ranch had grown at a phenomenal rate. In his church of a few hundred adults, at one point the youth group mushroomed to eight hundred teenagers. I longed to go to the Youth Ranch meetings with my big brother, Doug, who had also been dramatically impacted by Yankee's church. Although I was technically too young, I persistently begged and pleaded. "Don't worry; I'll sneak you in," Doug finally promised.

Even though there were seven years between us, Doug and I had a special bond as brothers. But that bond would be stressed and stretched in the coming months in ways I never imagined in my worst nightmares.

CHAPTER 13

"ALWAYS WIN SOLES"

"HEY, BIG BROTHER!" Doug said. Although he was several years older than I was, Doug called me "big brother."

"Why do you always call me big brother?" I asked. "I'm ten years old, and you're seventeen. You're *my* big brother."

"I call you big brother because you're smarter than me. You know the Bible better than me. I call you big brother because I look up to you," Doug said.

That felt really awkward.

What Doug didn't realize was that *I* was the one who looked up to *him*. While I had my own unique set of obstacles to overcome, Doug had even more. Still, in spite of it all, he seemed happy-go-lucky. Outwardly, at least.

Doug looked perfectly normal. A lot of girls thought he was good looking. His jet-black hair was always perfectly kempt.

His teeth were astoundingly white. And his smile—his smile would light up a room. But there was a monumental struggle building underneath this handsome facade.

Like tectonic plates colliding underneath the ocean floor that trigger an unstoppable tsunami, Doug's low self-image eventually smashed up against many of the same identity struggles I had. But Doug had medical challenges too.

"He's having another seizure!" Ma yelled, frantically running toward him.

I froze in fear.

In seconds, Doug collapsed with a *thunk* onto the bathroom floor of our small apartment.

The loud impact jolted me from my fear-induced stupor. I ran to our rotary phone and dialed 911. I knew the drill. Doug had been having seizures for as long as I could remember.

When I returned to the bathroom, Ma was sitting on the floor slapping Doug's face, trying desperately to revive him.

Doug's seizures could be bad—heart-stoppingly bad. Ma and I were both afraid that someday we'd lose him to one. His epilepsy treatment and medication were hit and miss. Mostly miss.

Seeing Ma so scared scared me, too. We waited, desperate for the EMTs to arrive.

Ma sent me to the door to let them in. But just as the EMTs rushed into the bathroom, Doug started to come back around. One EMT checked his pulse and took his blood pressure. The other pulled out a small flashlight to shine into Doug's eyes and check his pupils. His vitals had returned to normal. After observing him for a while, the EMTs thought he seemed stable enough, so they packed up their gear and left.

Ma and I looked at each other with relief—for now—but we both knew this scary scenario would be replayed again and again down the road.

School was hard for Doug too. "There's too many numbers in math, big brother. There's too many words in English," he told me repeatedly.

Teenagers with learning disabilities were considered dumb. This made Doug an easy target for coldhearted cruelty at his school. Other kids could be ruthless with their snarky comments, mean jokes, and out-and-out bullying.

And they often added injury to insult.

"What happened to you?" I asked Doug one afternoon when he came limping into the kitchen after school.

"I had a kid twice my size pick me up and throw me over the ledge at the top of the stairs on the second floor at school. I landed at the bottom of the steps, and all I did was sprain my ankle. It's my lucky day," he said, trying to make a joke of it.

But the look in his eyes said something different. I knew that look—it was shame. It was the same shame I felt deep down inside whenever someone was mean to me—like the time Uncle Dave gave me the doll for Christmas or whenever neighborhood kids bullied me on my way home from school.

Both Doug and I operated from a place of shame, assuming that if others were mean to us, it was our fault, not theirs. Other kids seemed to sense our insecurity.

We didn't measure up to the family standard. Neither of us was cut from the same strong, tough, ready-for-anything cloth as the rest of the family. It wasn't so much that we were physically weak. We just seemed weak compared to the rest of our bulky bloodline. And that left both of us feeling like inadequate misfits within our own family.

But instead of turning his insecurity and inadequacies inward, as I did, Doug began to push outward—to kick against the goads, to spit in eyes, to curse the darkness and swing at whatever was there.

"It's not the first time I've dropped my books in the middle of the hallway at school to fight some bully. Sometimes I win. Sometimes I lose. But I'm always up for a fight," Doug said, continuing his story.

One thing he had in common with our extended family was an explosive temper.

"But this time the kid was just too big for me. I wonder if I'll get expelled again this time for fighting," he said, peering intently at his sprained ankle, assessing the swelling.

Doug and I shared more than feelings of inadequacy and shame. Although both of us, at different times, had put our faith in Jesus as young kids at Bethany Baptist Church, we both had significant "daddy issues."

Our dad, George Stier, would call every once in a great while. Whenever I answered the phone, he would just say, "Put your brother on the line." He never wanted to talk to me. Even his conversations with Doug were always short and curt. I had no memory of him. He was the guy before the guy before Paul (of baseball bat fame), and he left my ma long before I was old enough to remember anything.

While I kept my father issues locked away deep inside, Doug unleashed his for all the world to see.

It all came to a hellish head one day as the bus dropped me off in front of our apartment complex after school. I couldn't believe my eyes. Two cop cars were parked in front of the apartment building. This looked exciting! There were several cops out on the lawn in front of the building too. But my excitement quickly turned to panic once I got a closer look. My brother, handcuffed and highly agitated, was being escorted toward one of the cop cars.

"Where are you taking my brother?" I screamed as I ran toward them.

"It's okay, big brother!" Doug said, trying to calm me. The cop holding his arm looked confused—I was half Doug's size, yet he'd called me "big brother." "It's okay," Doug repeated, tears streaming down his face.

Ma, collapsed to her knees on the grass, screamed, "Why, Doug? Why did you do it?" There were two cops next to her, trying to calm and comfort her.

But Ma was inconsolable. "Where are they taking him?" she yelled.

"Ma'am, they're just taking him into the police station for booking," one of the cops said gently.

But Ma knew what that meant. Our family was no stranger to police stations. Her oldest son was about to be arrested, booked, and thrown in jail. Pushing the cops away, she headed straight for her red Ford Pinto. Noticing me standing there on the sidewalk looking lost and confused, she said, "Greg, go and make yourself a TV dinner. I gotta go to the police station."

Ma peeled out of her parking spot and left the scene of the crime. But what crime?

As I made my way toward the apartment building, one of the remaining cops gave me a half-smile of pity. "What did my brother do?" I asked, worried that he had hurt someone.

"Your brother vandalized this apartment," the police officer said, pointing toward the open door of the apartment next to ours.

"I don't know what that word means," I said.

"He tore it apart—destroyed the couches and carpets, broke dishes, and ruined clothes," the cop explained. "We know he did it because he sprayed a fire extinguisher all over the place and got the white chemicals all over the carpet and on his shoes. When we knocked on the door of your apartment, we could see the white on his shoes. When we asked to have a closer look at his shoes, he confessed."

"Why did he do it?" I asked. "We like the family who lives there."

"I have no idea," the police officer said, shaking his head sadly.

Later that night, after I thought about it some, I concluded that I did know why he did it.

My grandma used to cook food in a big cooker that had some kind of whistle on top. I remember asking her, "Grandma, what is that thing on the top of the lid of that great big pot?"

"That pot," she explained, "is called a pressure cooker. When I cook the food in water, it eventually boils inside the pot. That creates steam, which creates pressure. When there's enough pressure, that little thing on the lid is like a whistle that releases the pressure and lets me know the food is ready."

"What would happen if you didn't have that thing on top?" I asked.

"Hmmm," she said. "Well, I suppose it would blow up!"

My brother had been in a pressure cooker without an escape valve. This was the blowup.

The hot water of his epilepsy, learning disabilities, and daddy issues was poured into the pot of violence in our family. Finally, the lid called mockery was locked into place. That lid had no escape valve. So it was just a matter of time before boil and *boom!*

But the people next door made a plea on Doug's behalf to the cops. They liked Doug and knew that he was just confused. They begged that he not be sent to juvenile hall.

Once at the police station, right before they booked my brother for destruction of property, they gave him a choice: "juvie" or an extended stay at the Mount Airy Psychiatric Hospital.

Doug and Ma chose Mount Airy.

Doug's being locked away in a mental hospital rocked me to the core. I was scared for Doug, but I was also scared for me. I was scared because we were blood. I was scared because, although in many ways we were very different, in many more ways we shared the same brand of insecurities and fears.

I overheard more than one conversation between Ma and my grandparents or Ma and one of my uncles. They were all talking about a film that had just come to the theaters that fall, *One Flew Over the Cuckoo's Nest*, which made it clear that a lot was seriously wrong with the current approach to psychiatric treatment. These conversations always ended abruptly whenever I entered the room. But even as a ten-year-old, it took only one visit to Mount Airy for me to realize that Doug was not in a good place.

The first time Ma and I visited Doug, I was really nervous. As we sat in the waiting room, I looked around me. It was stark and cold and bare. *Is this where I'm headed?* I wondered. Although Doug was battling a different set of giants, there was one Goliath we both struggled with—that ever-present feeling that we were misfits who didn't really belong in our rough, tough extended family.

While Ma and I waited for Doug to come down, I wanted to ask her if she thought I was going to have to come here someday too, but I dared not. Ma blamed herself for Doug's crime. Ever since Doug's violent outburst at the neighbors' apartment, she'd redoubled her old, "I'm a bum" mantra. Ma traced all this back to the sins of her not-too-distant past.

Doug walked through the door all dressed in white. He looked almost angelic. His dazzlingly white scrubs matched his brilliantly bright teeth. A large, intimidating man stood next to Doug during our entire visit, listening silently as Ma, Doug, and I made small talk. I don't know if he was bored to death from supervising guest visits or trained to maintain a neutral, passive presence, but he never reacted to anything we said.

We'd just finished talking about how bad the food was there when, abruptly, Doug leaned in closer to me and looked me straight in the eye. "Hey, big brother, I'm not crazy. These guys are crazy!" he said, motioning toward the door that led back toward the hospital ward. A small smile played across his face as he watched my confusion.

But once Ma laughed out loud at Doug's comment, I relaxed some.

"Whaddya mean?" I asked innocently.

"One girl, I think she's demon-possessed, ran and jumped out a glass window, but she survived," he explained. "After she recovered, they brought her back in with the rest of us."

"Yeah, then what happened?" I asked, distressed by the

reference to demons, since I'd been wondering for years whether the devil was after me.

"She was glaring at me from across the room, and even though the lights were low, I could see her red eyes and hear her growling threats at me in some kind of demon voice," Doug said casually. He seemed almost nonchalant, but I was terrified for him.

"What did you do?" Ma asked.

"I started singing 'Amazing Grace' louder and louder. The louder I got, the louder she got. It was getting everyone riled up," Doug continued, "so I finally asked all the other patients in the room to join in the song. And they did! Eventually the hospital staff took her away because she was out of control.

"I'm sure glad I have Jesus here with me. I couldn't handle it in here without him. I mean, I know I got problems, but these poor people locked away here who don't have Jesus, they've got really, really big problems."

Doug told me later that after he left us and went back up to his room, he went to his second-story window and watched Ma and me walking to our car. We had turned around for one final look back at the hospital and seen Doug in the window. He waved at us, and we waved back.

"For some reason," Doug recounted later, "I knew right then that it was going to all be okay. I knew that I was done with trying to please myself and would spend the rest of my life serving God."

Day after day passed, and I missed my brother. Soon days turned to weeks and weeks into months and months into wondering if he would ever be set free.

But Doug's six-month stint in the mental institute sealed and steeled his faith. He dived into Scripture. He shared the gospel with the other patients and the doctors, with the custodians and the secretaries—with anyone and everyone.

He came out of Mount Airy on fire for God in all the right ways.

Afterward, while I watched hour after hour of television in our little apartment, Doug was reading his Bible for hours on end. It made me feel guilty.

Every thirty minutes or so, he'd come up to me during a commercial, point to a passage of Scripture and ask, "What does this mean, big brother?" After I'd explain it to him, he'd thank me and go back to reading. This happened again and again and again.

But for Doug, it wasn't just about reading the Bible; he was sharing its message with others. Doug was relentless about sharing the gospel, and he loved to drag me along with him when he went looking for people to share with.

One Saturday morning—my one day of the week to sleep in—Doug was leaning down over my bed, insistently shaking my shoulder.

Why is he trying to rouse me out of my deep, comfortable, Saturday-morning sleep?

"Wake up, Greg! Wake up! Let's go tell someone about Jesus!" he said, urgently pulling the covers off me. "No, don't just roll over and go back to sleep. Wake up!"

"It's kind of early," I said groggily, glancing up at the clock. "I think most everyone is still sleeping." It was barely past 7 a.m., but Doug would not be deterred.

"We gotta go now, Greg! There are so many people out there who need to hear about Jesus! Get up!"

"Okay, okay," I said resignedly, sitting up and swinging my feet onto the cold, hard floor. "Let me get some breakfast first, though."

After I got dressed, Doug settled into a chair across the kitchen table from me, watching me like a hawk, begrudging every spoonful of Cocoa Puffs I downed.

"Let's go now!" he said. "People are dying and going to hell, and we need to put a stop to it!"

"Okay, I guess," I said, rolling my eyes. He'd just ruined my last few spoonfuls of Cocoa Puffs by sprinkling them with a dusting of guilt.

Once outside, we walked and walked, looking for someone —anyone—to talk to about Jesus. The longer we walked around looking, the more frustrated Doug got. He was visibly agitated. His face and neck were bright red, a sure sign he was upset.

Finally, out of sheer frustration, Doug screamed, "Where is everyone?"

"They're still in bed like normal people. It's Saturday morning," I explained.

But Doug wasn't ready to give up. "Let's try over at the park," he said.

We walked side by side in silence until the park came into view.

"There's one!" Doug shouted, pointing at what looked to be an eight-year-old boy playing on the jungle gym. Then Doug took off sprinting straight toward the kid at full speed. "I'll get him!" he yelled, oblivious to what this might look like to the kid or a random bystander.

The kid froze in fear as Doug closed the distance. Before

he even got to the kid, Doug yelled, "Hey, kid! Where are you going when you *die?*"

I suspect the last word of the question was the only word the kid heard. The poor boy took off running as fast as his little legs would carry him.

Doug turned abruptly and headed back toward me, his shoulders slumped in despair.

"You scared that kid to death," I said. "You can't do that, Doug."

"I didn't mean to, big brother," he said, tears springing to his eyes. "I just don't want to see that kid go to hell. I want him to know Jesus like I know Jesus, like you know Jesus."

I wondered whether Doug's newfound enthusiasm for evangelism would wane with time. But it didn't. Instead, it escalated. He bought a bicycle and rode it everywhere, talking to every pedestrian he met. Once he told me that he pulled up to a car at a red light and began sharing the gospel with the car full of guys. When the light turned green, they said, "We gotta go, man." But Doug wasn't quite done explaining the gospel, so he grabbed the car door handle and said, "Go ahead and drive, and I'll finish explaining the gospel to you." And 45 miles per hour later, once he'd finally finished telling them the Good News of Jesus, he let go of the car and coasted to safety.

There was nobody Doug wouldn't talk to. And more often than not—once he learned not to run toward or yell at people— his ultra-sincere manner and his ear-to-ear smile drew people in like a tractor beam. They genuinely listened. In spite of his limited vocabulary, he had an unlimited joy, and that was more than enough.

When I was a teenager, Doug wrote me a letter, exhorting me to share the gospel. "Always win soles!" he wrote.

Although he was a horrible speller, he was an amazing soul winner.

Doug became legendary at Yankee's church and at Youth Ranch for his evangelistic boldness. And, in many ways, I was grateful for that. It seemed like *my* big brother had found his purpose. But his newfound focus also frustrated me.

Doug seemed to finally have a clear direction in life—but I didn't. *Despite all the times I've almost died, I'm still here. Why?* I wondered. *What am I called to do? Why am I here? What am I supposed to do with my life?* Doug knew, but I was still clueless.

Little did I know that I was about to take a bus trip across the nation that would start to answer my haunting questions.

CHAPTER 14

THE ROAD TRIP

"WELCOME TO YOUTH RANCH!" Yankee said in his backwoods Georgia accent before leading the crowd in a hillbilly version of "I'll Fly Away."

Backing him up was "The Firehouse Five." Bob Daly, the guy who had stayed in the car when Yankee was sharing Jesus with my uncle Jack, was on the electric guitar. The other band members were mostly teenagers. One played the bongos while others played acoustic guitars. There was even a bass made from an old washtub turned upside down and connected to a string and a stick.

What an anomaly. Here was a man nicknamed Yankee who spoke with a Southern accent leading a bunch of suburban and urban kids from metro Denver in singing country-western-sounding Christian songs. But it worked.

The place was packed with hundreds of loud, crazy, hot, smelly teenagers. There was a one-hundred-foot banana split melting in a long gutter trough. "Sometimes they order pizzas by the truckload," Doug informed me as we dug in and did our part to devour the ice cream.

The meeting was peppered with testimonies and skits, as well. But the highlight was when the Word was opened and Yankee unpacked Scripture.

My first meeting, like every other meeting I ever attended, culminated in a clear explanation of the gospel and a passionate, bow-your-heads, close-your-eyes, raise-your-hand appeal to respond to Christ. The best I can remember, from the first time I went to Youth Ranch as a pre-junior-higher until I graduated from high school, at least one person trusted in Jesus every meeting. Usually there were several new believers.

Witnessing so many teens respond to the gospel moved me, and I soon began to invite others to Youth Ranch too.

But I wasn't content with just a weekly meeting. I wanted more. This same gospel that had infused Uncle Jack and Uncle Bob with passion and purpose was starting to stir something down deep inside of me.

But it was more than that. For the first time, I was part of a secure community of believers who were on mission and had a purpose, consumed with love for God and with his love for us. There was something there I hadn't felt in my grandparents' little Baptist church. It was a love that was beckoning me, calling me to God on a deeper level. I could almost taste it, and I wanted more.

One night, one of the youth leaders announced, "This August, we'll be taking a group of junior and senior highers to Hollywood, Florida, for a weeklong camp at Florida Bible College."

At that time, junior high consisted of seventh and eighth grades. I'd just finished fifth grade. I wasn't even supposed to be attending Youth Ranch (Doug sneaked me in), so I was way too young to be considered as a candidate for the FBC Camp. Still, I was desperate to go and learn more about Jesus and about reaching others for him. And I had enough Mathias blood in me that once I locked in on something, I wouldn't give up.

After much convincing, the youth leaders made an exception to the seventh-grade rule just for me. I couldn't wait to experience camp with the big kids! Plus, I was curious to see how Bible college had changed Uncle Bob, who was still a student at FBC. While getting ready for camp, I realized something that surprised me. I missed my uncle Bob. He was such a different person from my earliest recollections of him. He was no longer the beast of earlier years. He was, well, just Uncle Bob. And I couldn't wait to see him.

The last of our luggage had been stowed in the back of the bus. Kenny Sanchez, the youth-leader-turned-bus-driver, stood up in the center of the sweltering school bus and announced, "This is going to be a long road trip from Denver to Hollywood, Florida, so get comfortable and have fun. Just don't do anything stupid." Then he led us in prayer, and we were on our way.

Being the youngest on the bus, I was kind of quiet at first. These were high schoolers and junior highers, and I was technically still in elementary school. Plus, most of these teenagers came from middle-class families. I felt out of place and insecure on more than one level.

But before long, I was joking around with the rest of them. From pillow fights to food fights to actual fights, even day one of that bus ride was a long one. But as evening darkened the sky, Richie Martinez took his guitar out and started leading us in some Youth Ranch songs.

He started with "Oh, You'll Never Get to Heaven." He led the fun lyrics, and we echoed back.

Oh, you'll never get to heaven
On roller skates,
'Cause you'll roll right by
Those pearly gates.

Oh, you'll never get to heaven
In Yankee's car,
'Cause Yankee's car
Won't go that far.

As the song went on, others started making up lyrics and leading the sing-along while Richie continued to strum.

Oh, you'll never get to heaven
Smoking pot,
'Cause you'll think you're there
But you're really not!

After a few more fun songs, Richie shifted gears and led us in more serious worship songs. As we lifted our voices in unison to "Amazing Grace" and "Pass It On," these slower songs not only spiritually prepared us for the coming week but also readied us for at least an attempt at getting some sleep during the overnight bus ride.

Around midnight, the hiss of the air brakes signaled one last late-night fill-'er-up at the truck stop. While Kenny filled up the gas tank, the kids who were still awake—which was most of us—filled up on junk food. Except for me. I didn't have enough extra spending money to buy a late-night Twinkie.

As I climbed the three big steps back onto the bus, Kenny said, "Wait a minute, Greg, I want to talk to you about something." He motioned me into the spot directly behind the driver's seat.

When the last teenager had climbed aboard, Kenny walked the bus aisle and, starting from the back, quietly counted the number of people on board. Leaving someone behind during a pit stop was a youth leader's worst nightmare.

While he counted, my mind raced. *What does Kenny want to talk to me about? Did I already do or say something wrong? Is he upset that Yankee let an elementary school kid go to a teenagers-only camp?*

My insecurities had reared their ugly head. *I don't fit into my muscle-bound family, and maybe I don't fit into this Florida-bound youth group either.*

"And Greg is number forty-five," Kenny said under his breath before plopping down into the driver's seat.

"Here we go," he said as the bus rolled away from the truck stop and back onto the road that led to the highway.

I sat there quiet, hoping he would forget I was sitting behind him. I wanted nothing more than to slink back to my original seat and get some sleep.

But once on the highway, Kenny said abruptly, "Greg, I'm gonna ask you to do me a favor."

"Okay," I said hesitantly, not knowing what to expect.

"I have a long drive ahead of me, and I really need someone who can talk to me and keep me awake all night. I was wondering if you would do that for me?"

"Sure," I said, surprised and relieved that I wasn't in trouble for something.

Over the next six hours until sunrise, we talked and talked. He asked about my family and told me about his. He asked me how I had come to Christ and shared about his spiritual journey to Jesus. He asked me about my relationship with the Lord. Then he asked me a question that brought me up short.

"What do you want to do for God someday?" Kenny asked.

Do for God? What can I do for God?

"I dunno," I said, honestly. "I never thought about it that way."

"God has called you for a purpose," Kenny said like a wise old sage, even though he was only in his early twenties. "I can see it. God wants to use you in a great way."

I looked around me to see if he was talking to someone else. But everyone else was asleep.

As the hours ticked by, Kenny talked to me about developing "a burden for souls" and becoming a "soul winner." He challenged me to serve God with everything I had. He talked to me like I was an adult at church, not an eleven-year-old kid from the hood.

By the time the sun rose above Missouri's rolling hills, for the first time in my life I felt like God must have a purpose for me. But what it was, I had no idea.

After a thirty-three-hour road trip in an un-air-conditioned church bus, we arrived at Florida Bible College hot and sweaty but excited. Two thousand teenagers from all across the country—plus one soon-to-be sixth grader—crowded into the auditorium. The energy in the room was palpable.

There were hilarious skits, amazing music, and powerful testimonies of gospel-transformed lives, mostly given by Florida Bible College students.

Every night, we were challenged to live and share our faith. Every morning, we were equipped to share the gospel. And every afternoon, we had the opportunity to put into practice the evangelism training we'd just received.

Years earlier, Ray Stanford had raised the money to purchase the historic Hollywood Beach Hotel and convert it into Florida Bible College. The college owned the long strip of beachfront behind the school that was situated right on the Hollywood boardwalk.

After the morning sessions and lunch, we'd all pour out onto the huge beach to play in the warm water and share Jesus with those walking by on the boardwalk.

After the nighttime meetings, I'd go back to my dorm room to get some sleep. My roommate? Uncle Bob—the monster I used to run and hide from was now my "roomie" at FBC!

"What did you learn today?" he would ask. And I would enthusiastically share the amazing things I'd learned and experienced.

By the end of camp, when I looked around at the thousands of teenagers who'd been equipped to share the gospel, I felt like I was part of an unstoppable movement—a movement that had changed my own life and was changing the trajectory of my crazy violent family.

Although I didn't know it at the time, a seed was planted in me that week that would one day grow into a global vision for reaching teenagers around the world with the gospel.

CHAPTER 15

I SAW THE SIGN

"GREG, I HAVE A LITTLE HOMEWORK ASSIGNMENT for you,"
Timo told me one night at Youth Ranch. A slight, knowing
smile played across his dark, thin, chiseled face as he watched
for my reaction.

"Timo" was Tim's nickname. He was one of the infamous
Sanchez brothers who, at different times, worked with Yankee to
pull off Youth Ranch. Both Timo and his older brother, Kenny,
the bus driver, had committed their lives to Christ as a result of
Yankee's Youth Ranch ministry in Arvada. Both of them had a
passion to reach and disciple teenagers in the same way they had
been reached and discipled through Yankee's ministry.

Neither Timo, Kenny, nor I was from Arvada—a middle-
class, mostly white suburb northwest of Denver. The three of
us hailed from the rougher, tougher urban core of the metro

area, giving us a special affinity beyond our common faith. This affinity extended to the Archuleta and Martinez siblings as well. It was urban grit combined with a passion to reach the lost that made our unity something special.

"Every soul is precious," Yankee preached. "In Luke 4:18, Jesus said, 'The Spirit of the Lord is upon me, because he hath anointed me to preach the gospel to the poor; he hath sent me to heal the brokenhearted, to preach deliverance to the captives, and recovering of sight to the blind, to set at liberty them that are bruised.'"

In Yankee's experience, poor kids like me generally responded to the gospel more readily, so he focused much of the church's outreach efforts on the apartment complexes, trailer courts, and cracker-box houses in the roughest parts of the city. The poorer, more marginalized, and more oppressed someone was, the more open they tended to be to the good news of Jesus.

That's how Yankee saw it. That's how I saw it. That's how my family saw it.

Jesus' message and mission unified us all. On the streets—before trusting Christ—my uncles would have seen the Sanchez brothers as enemies. But in this church, after Jesus, we all were united together in the love of God for the cause of Christ.

As a middle schooler, I was increasingly attuned to the Italian/Hispanic racial tensions that simmered in my old neighborhood, often to the point of boiling over. So the change in Uncle Jack's and Uncle Bob's attitudes toward their Hispanic brothers and sisters in Christ grabbed my attention like a flashing neon sign. It occurred to me that perhaps Jesus' message was the key to obliterating racism.

But even more attention-getting than my uncles' striking

shift in attitude was the fact that many of the youth group leaders who impacted me spiritually were Hispanic—including Timo.

Although Timo was barely out of high school himself, his passion for sharing the gospel was uncontainable. And he had a plan for kindling that same kind of passion inside me.

"What homework assignment?" I asked, sighing. As a twelve-year-old attending Yankee's little Christian school, I had my fill of books to read and papers to write. Arvada Christian School was *way* harder than the public school I had previously attended.

"I want you to go to the mall this Saturday night and sit on a bench in the busiest part," Timo said.

"Okay . . ." I said hesitantly, expecting him to deliver some sort of punchline where the joke was on me.

But Timo wasn't joking. "I want you to sit there for thirty minutes and watch people."

That sounds kinda creepy.

"And as you watch them," Timo continued, "I want you to put an imaginary tag on their foreheads that reads 'Bound for Hell.'"

Okay, that's not creepy. That's just weird.

When Timo saw my face twist into a question mark, he said, "People who die without responding to the gospel spend an eternity in hell. Jesus described hell as a place of eternal darkness, suffering, and regret. So I want you to take that in. As hard as it may be, I want you to watch people for thirty minutes and imagine them being separated from God in hell forever, without hope of escape."

As a result of all those Sundays I'd spent attending my grandparents' Baptist church, hell was always hovering over my head like an axe of guilt ready to drop. So Timo's words stirred something down deep inside me. But I wasn't quite sure what.

"Will you take this challenge, Greg?" Timo asked. It felt like his narrowed eyes were peering straight into my soul.

"Yes, I will," I declared, ready to take the dare. My family would never back down from a challenge, and maybe I had some of their hutzpah after all.

When Saturday night rolled around, Ma dropped me off at the new Westminster Mall, which pulsated with people on Friday and Saturday nights. It was the new weekend gathering spot for teenagers looking to flirt, play video games in the arcade, and sometimes fight. Ma assumed I was there to hang out with friends.

The mall, which still smelled of new construction, spilled out in four directions from a central common area that featured a large, sunken, rectangular pool, which served as the hub of the mall's foot traffic. I made a beeline for this gathering spot. Settling in on an empty bench, I took in my surroundings.

Over the pool hovered four multicolored, five-foot-tall hot-air balloons that gently rose to the ceiling and descended back down to the water beneath, guided by a single wire. In front of the pool, ascending stairstep levels of seating served as a social gathering spot for families, couples, and teenagers. The seating area provided a respite in the midst of the noisy, crowded shopping craziness. It was a place to sit, relax, and catch your breath while watching the mesmerizing mini hot-air balloons float up and down. Occasionally someone would approach the pool's edge and toss a coin in for good luck.

It was time to begin my homework assignment. Looking

down at the cheap Timex watch strapped to my wrist, I noted the time.

As I turned my gaze from the balloons to the people, a flush of nervousness swept through me. *What if the people I'm watching notice me watching them? They'll think I'm some kind of weirdo.* So I tried to look like I wasn't looking by casting occasional averting glances around me before nervously averting my eyes—no doubt making me look even more suspicious.

This is super awkward. Still, I have an assignment from Timo, and I said I'd do it. So I stuck with it. After a few minutes, my tween awkwardness began to fade. I looked more intently at the people walking by.

A mom holding a J.C. Penney shopping bag was being pulled by her preschooler toward the Orange Julius shop. My mouth watered at the thought of the best smoothies ever.

A young couple slowly strolled toward me hand in hand, almost floating in their own world. They headed toward the jewelry store. Maybe they were looking at engagement rings.

A tall, acned teenager with greasy, shoulder-length hair walked past in a long black trench coat. *If I wasn't from North Denver, I would think he looks scary.*

But that cocky voice of bravado inside my head didn't really sound like *me*. It sounded like my family BC (before Christ). Deep down inside—if I was honest with myself—my voice *wasn't* confident or courageous. It was intimidated and confused. My fatherlessness had left me insecure, with a gaping hole in my heart. That doll Uncle Dave had given me years ago still haunted me. All those hours spent cowering behind the couch or under the sink while Uncle Bob ranted and raved had left me spooked and scarred. All my run-ins with death had left me full of questions about life and God's purpose for me. Despite my faith in Christ and my all-night talk with Kenny on the long bus ride to Florida, I still had no clear idea who I was or what purpose God had for me.

But this homework assignment was helping me to find a different voice—my true voice—a voice of purpose and potential.

To quiet the confusing, conflicting voices in my head, I sent up a quick, silent prayer. *Father, help me see people like you see them, like Jesus sees them. As weird as this exercise feels, God, help me to see the sign.*

Immediately, Matthew 9:36—a memory verse—popped into my head: "When he saw the crowds, he had compassion on them, because they were harassed and helpless, like sheep without a shepherd."

Had the Father given his Son the homework assignment of watching people too? Timo had told me to visualize the sign "Bound for Hell" on each person. But when Jesus saw the crowds, he didn't just see the hell they were headed to but also the one they were going through right at that very moment. He saw them as "harassed and helpless, like sheep without a shepherd."

I thought back to the one time I'd seen a sheep without a shepherd. I was seven years old. Grandpa and I were fishing along a mountain stream when Grandpa sent me up through the woods to the Ford F-150 truck to get some more fishing tackle.

Across my years of camping with Grandma and Grandpa, they'd repeatedly warned me about the many different kinds of dangerous wild animals that roamed the Rockies. So as I set off on my solo trip back to the truck, I was nervous about encountering a bear or a mountain lion whose open jaws could swallow me whole. I tentatively made my way through the pine trees and up the steep hill. But when I climbed the final embankment before my last push to the road on top, I was shocked to encounter a different kind of animal. There in the wilds of the Rocky Mountains was a little lost lamb.

The lamb froze in fear, and so did I. Within a second or two the lamb snapped to, turned, and ran. I knew this lamb was not supposed to be running loose in the wild. It would soon be a victim of one of the same fanged predators I'd been taught to fear. So in a spurt of rare "courage," I chased it, hoping to catch it and take it to my grandpa. He'd know how to help it. Grandpa knew everything.

But the little lamb ran surprisingly fast, and it quickly disappeared into the forest. I stopped and sadly turned back toward the truck. Even I knew that poor little lamb would likely be dead soon.

Lambs really are defenseless. As my thoughts shifted back to the people walking past me at the mall, I sensed what my memory verse was talking about. These people—like that little lamb I'd encountered in the mountains—would someday die. Some sooner, some later. But eventually all of them would die. And once they did, it would be too late to save their lost souls from hell.

My mind drifted back through my own close calls with death—my slit wrists from the window accident, my ruptured appendix, the dog attack, plus I'd recently had one more brush with death. Now I was up to four near-death experiences in my short life.

The grim reaper was like an aggressive salesman who repeatedly knocked at my door, trying to close the deal. On each of these occasions, my hand was on the doorknob, ready to let him in, when God intervened to chase him away.

As I sat there on the bench in the mall, with thoughts of death and dying swirling around me, I thought about my most recent run-in with the grim reaper.

We were living in our apartment in a low-rent district in the suburb of Westminster, the same one where Doug had been arrested. Ma had moved us there to be closer to her work, but now that Grandma and Grandpa's house was farther away and Doug was gone too, serving his six-month stint in a mental institution, I was a latchkey kid for a few hours every day after school.

On this particular day, I had let myself in our apartment door and shed my backpack to the floor.

Should I watch TV or just start doing homework?

The TV beckoned. I was crossing the room to switch it on when I first saw the culprit in a glass bowl sitting right in the middle of our kitchen table.

Ma didn't keep a ton of candy around the house, but somehow one lone piece of hard butterscotch candy had escaped everyone's notice. Without thinking twice, I unwrapped the candy and popped it into my mouth.

But it didn't land in my mouth. Instead, it hurtled past my mouth and straight into my windpipe. In that moment, everything stopped—including my breathing.

It felt like someone had taken a pair of pliers and completely cut off my air supply.

I couldn't gasp.

I couldn't wheeze.

I couldn't breathe.

Ma wouldn't be home for hours. Panic hit me like the bloodstained baseball bat we kept behind the door.

I rushed toward the phone to call 911. *But wait*, I thought. *Even if I call 911, I can't say anything with a butterscotch candy lodged in my windpipe. Surely they won't send help if I can't tell them what's wrong.*

What about the next-door neighbors? If one of them is home, they'll help me!

I ran out of our front door and knocked furiously on the neighbor's door.

Nobody was home.

I was getting light-headed. *What are my other options? Run to the street and wave a car down!*

So that's what I tried. But no cars were coming.

Panicking, I literally ran in circles. It'd been at least a full minute since I'd taken a breath. I was close to blacking out.

If something doesn't happen quickly, I thought, *I'm going to die a very embarrassing death—death by butterscotch candy.*

But wait—I haven't knocked on the door of the One who can actually save me!

So I stopped running in circles and knocked at the door of heaven in prayer. *God, if you don't show me what to do right now, I'm going to die. Please show me what to do.*

While I have never heard the audible voice of God, in that moment a thought was planted in my ten-year-old brain.

Stand on your head.

Instantly my heart was calm, although my head was feeling

lighter and lighter as my body's oxygen level moved lower and lower.

But right there, on the little grass patch in front of our apartment building, I bent over, put the crown of my head onto the ground, placed my hands flat on the grass, and pushed my feet into the air.

If this doesn't work, I'll soon be unconscious. And then I'll be dead.

But as soon as my body went perpendicular, my windpipe unkinked and gravity did its work. That troublesome oblong piece of yellow butterscotch candy came sliding out of my windpipe and landed back in my mouth.

Coughing and wheezing, I collapsed on the ground and spit the mucous-covered candy into my hand. As I sucked huge breaths of air into my oxygen-depleted lungs, my brain and body kicked back into gear.

Sitting up, I looked at the slimy candy in my hand. *You almost killed me!* Then in an act of revenge, my open mouth met with my open palm and I crunched down hard, finishing the piece of candy that had tried to finish me.

As the traumatic memory faded, my thoughts snapped back to Westminster Mall and the people walking past me. I had eluded death four times because God had saved me. As a follower of Jesus, I didn't have to fear death. But I thought, *I'll be in heaven when I die. But what about all these people around me who don't have this same hope of heaven? Are they ready to die? How many brushes with death have they had? And when they do inevitably die, will they be in heaven or in hell? What will hell be like for them? Is Timo right? Will it be eternal darkness, flames, torment, and regret?*

The veil over the eternal was thinning for me.

One by one, I looked at the people walking by. *They're like sheep without a shepherd.* For the first time, I saw the sign—"Bound for Hell."

I saw it on the heads of the three Pomona High School football players strutting by in their letter jackets. I saw it on the forehead of that tall, scary-looking teenager who was on his second circuit around the mall.

I saw it on the forehead of every person who passed by me.

And with that sign, I saw the flames. I saw the pain. I saw the hopelessness. Eventually, I closed my eyes, but I continued to imagine that sign on the heads of the people I heard walking by.

After several minutes, I opened my eyes. They stung from the salty tears that poured down my cheeks. As I wiped my face, my heart was fully broken.

Looking at each passerby, I imagined the hole in their soul that they were trying to fill with more, with bigger, with better—with something, with anything other than the God who loved them.

How sad they must feel when they lay their heads down on their beds each night! I thought. *Or maybe they don't feel it. Maybe they just sense the slow pain of meaninglessness that's eating away at the fabric of their souls one day at a time.*

I looked down at my watch. More than thirty minutes had passed. My homework assignment was complete.

Then I knew why Doug was so passionate about reaching lost souls. I knew why Yankee fearlessly reached out to my family with the gospel so many years ago.

Their mission was to rescue the lost at any cost.

Could this be the reason God has spared my life again and

again? I wondered. There was something about this mission that resonated with me on a deeper-than-I-had-ever-felt level.

My brushes with death had brushed me up against the eternal. Now I had peered into the abyss, and it had changed me.

"Hey, Timo," I said the next day at church. "I did the homework assignment. I imagined the 'Bound for Hell' sign on people's foreheads for thirty minutes at the mall last night."

"And?" Timo asked.

"It worked," I said simply.

The Lego pieces were beginning to click into place in my soul. But there was still a piece missing, although I hadn't realized it until Ma sat me down and told me a story.

CHAPTER 16

"SIT DOWN, I WANT TO TELL YOU SOMETHING"

BRRRINNNG! The phone was annoyingly loud. Since I was the closest, I grabbed the receiver.

"Hello!" I said in my high-pitched twelve-year-old-boy voice.

"Shirley?" a man on the other end of the line growled.

"No, this is Greg, her son," I said, correcting the unknown caller with a twinge of embarrassment creeping into my voice.

"You sound like a girl," the man declared matter-of-factly. But before I could protest, he continued, "This is George Stier. Let me talk to your brother."

There it was again: a double-barreled shotgun of insult. First, he told me I sounded like a girl, and then, once again, he wanted to talk to my brother—not me.

"Doug!" I yelled, trying to lower my Vienna Boys' Choir pitch down to a bass, or at least a baritone.

I handed the phone to Doug. "It's George Stier," I said. I never used the word *dad* when talking about him. It just didn't sound right.

While Doug launched into his conversation with George, I marched over to Ma. She was sitting at our round, white kitchen table smoking. She was halfway through her first pack of Benson and Hedges Golds, and the day was still young. I stood awkwardly next to her for a moment, summoning my courage.

"Ma, can I ask you a question about something that's really bothering me?"

"Sure. What?" she said turning toward me while contorting her lips so that her cigarette smoke blew off toward the refrigerator instead of toward me. Ma—like most other smokers of her day—wouldn't have dreamed of stepping outside to light up. She did, however, usually exercise the common courtesy of not blowing her cancer cloud straight at you.

"Why does George Stier never want to talk to me?" I demanded. "When he calls, he only wants to talk to Doug!" When she didn't reply, I forged ahead. "And why do you always call him 'Doug's dad'? He's my dad too! He hates me, but he's my dad."

Ma looked away from me uncomfortably and fixed her gaze straight ahead. She took a long drag from her cigarette, then exhaled. But this time she blew the smoke straight ahead across the table. It was almost as if she was looking at someone sitting there across from her. Someone she wanted to take direct aim at.

"Sit down. I want to tell you something," she said, turning her gaze back toward me and drilling into me with her piercing, sad blue eyes.

Nervously, I pulled a chair out from the table and sat down. I sensed I was about to learn something I didn't really want to know—but that I needed to know.

Ma ground out her cigarette in the giant green ashtray. Then she swallowed hard. Staring straight into my eyes, she said, "George Stier is not your father. Your father's name is Toney Woods. I met him at . . ." Ma continued to talk, but I'd stopped listening. Like a hard punch to your solar plexus that drops you to your knees and leaves you breathless—my uncle Jack had taught me that—I felt like the oxygen had left my lungs.

I must have heard her wrong.

Gathering my wits, I asked, "Ma, what did you just say?"

"George Stier is not your dad. Your dad's name is Toney Woods," she said articulating each word slowly and loudly, irritated that I'd made her repeat a truth she'd been trying to hide for over a decade.

"Where is he?" I asked.

"He's dead," she said.

"Why did he leave us?" I demanded.

"I don't really want to talk about it, Greg!" she barked. "It's hard enough to tell you this without dragging up all the details!"

"Ma!" I yelled, "You kept this a secret from me for all these years, and you wait until I'm twelve to tell me this?"

Normally, Ma wouldn't take this kind of verbal berating from anyone, but this time she just looked down at the table and kept smoking. But I wasn't done. I could feel the anger rising up inside me.

"All these years I thought George Stier was my dad. You gave me his last name!" I yelled. "No wonder he never wanted to talk to me! I'm *not* his son! And now you don't want to tell me about my real dad because it brings up bad memories for you! Well, too bad, Ma!"

In all my years, I had never talked to my ma like this, but I was beyond furious. I was enraged. Yet instead of grabbing me or slapping me or threatening me, she just sat there silently puffing on her cigarette, shame clearly written across her face.

Then it hit me. *All of this has ramifications far beyond who my dad is. It means my brother isn't really my full-blooded brother.* My anger drained away and an overwhelming sadness swept through me.

Tears spilled out of my eyes and rolled down my cheeks.

"I'm sorry to tell you like this, Greg," Ma said gently, putting her hand on my shoulder in a feeble effort to console me. "I should have told you this years ago, but I didn't know what to say."

But I was beyond comforting. I sobbed uncontrollably.

"Are you upset that George Stier is not your dad?" Ma asked.

"No!" I said between sobs. "This means Doug and I aren't full-blooded brothers! He's not my real brother!"

Doug was off the phone and had been listening quietly from the corner of the kitchen. "I'm your brother, you dork," he said in his no-nonsense way.

And somehow, I was comforted. His blunt words helped me think more clearly.

Full-blooded or not, he is my real brother.

Ma got up and grabbed me a couple of tissues. By the time I finished blowing my nose, my sobbing subsided. I pulled myself together. Now I was curious instead of crushed.

"Tell me more about my dad, Ma," I pleaded. "What was he like? What did he do? What did he look like?" But Ma didn't have many answers, so she offered a compromise. "I tell you what," she said. "Toney's sister-in-law, Tess, lives here in town. We keep in contact. I'll see if we can go to her house, and you can ask her whatever you want."

Ma got up, walked over to the rotary phone, looked up Tess's number in the little book she kept next to it, and dialed.

"Hey, Tess, this is Shirley," she said, like she was talking to an old friend.

The room went quiet while Ma listened to Tess on the other end of the line.

"Yeah, I'm doing good. You?" Ma said.

Although I could faintly hear the sound of Tess's voice, I couldn't make out what she was saying.

"Well, I just told Greg about Toney, and he's got questions," Ma said, glancing in my direction. "He's pretty upset."

You got that right!

"Can we all get together, and maybe he can ask you some questions about Toney?" Ma asked.

I heard Tess's muffled reply. "Sure," she said.

A thrill of excitement went through me.

"How about next Saturday night?" Ma asked.

"Sure," Tess said again.

Over the next week, the hours ticked by slowly. It was like waiting for Christmas to hurry up and get here. Saturday night would be an unveiling, like wrapping paper being stripped away, piece by piece, until you discovered the surprise inside. Hopefully, the visit with Tess would provide answers to some of the big questions that had been swirling around inside me for years. *Who am I really? And* whose *am I really?*

On Saturday night, Ma and I pulled into Tess's driveway.

Silently, we got out of the car and walked to the door. Ma pushed the doorbell and waited. It seemed like minutes, though it was probably just a matter of seconds before Tess opened the door.

"Shirley!" Tess said in greeting.

"Tess, how are you?" Ma asked.

"Pretty good. Come on in! And this must be Greg," she said, smothering me in an uncomfortably long hug. "He looks like you both!"

"I know, I know. He's got his dad's nose," Ma said.

Tess handed me a Coke and said, "Why don't you sit over there and watch TV while your mom and I catch up? Then you can join us and ask me any questions you want about your dad."

I quietly made my way over to the television, but I wasn't alone. There was another kid there whose name I didn't know. He didn't acknowledge my presence in any way, even though I sat down just three feet from him.

Tess and Ma took their seats in the little kitchenette across the room. They lit up cigarettes, drank coffee, and caught up. It was obvious that, at some point, they had been really good friends. After a few minutes, they lowered their voices to almost a whisper. I strained to hear what they were saying, but the TV was too loud. I guessed they were hatching a coordinated plan about how much to tell me about my father.

Since I couldn't hear what they were saying and the TV program was boring, I turned my attention to the other kid. It didn't take me long to conclude that he had significant intellectual disabilities, but what he was doing was more interesting than what was on TV.

The kid, who must have been related to me somehow, was playing with a contraption that consisted of two socks tied to a stick. Both socks were weighted with something inside them. Each time he spun the socks on the stick, he would emit sounds of excitement that culminated in a yell of pure delight. The faster the socks spun around on the stick, the more excited he got. Somehow, the weighted socks looked like they were rotating in opposite directions. It was totally baffling to me how that was even possible.

It suddenly struck me how strange this situation was. On one side of the room sat this boy who was absolutely exhilarated to watch his homemade toy spin, while on the other side of the room, my birth, life, dad, identity, and personal history were being discussed by the only two women on the planet who knew the real story.

"Greg, come over here," Ma finally said.

The other kid paid no attention to my departure. He just kept spinning and yelling with delight.

I made my way over to my ma and Tess.

"I have something to show you," Tess said. She handed me a carefully preserved newspaper article. "Your dad was a war hero."

She's exaggerating, of course, I thought.

I sat down between her and Ma and looked closer at the clipping in my hand. My eyes were immediately drawn to the photograph. It was a picture of my dad riding in the back of an open car in the middle of a ticker-tape parade.

Maybe she isn't exaggerating.

I started reading the article. The further I read, the more impressed I was. Toney Woods, my biological father, was not just a veteran of the Korean War. He was the very last prisoner of war to be released from captivity after the war was over. He'd spent three years in the worst possible conditions as a POW.

"When your dad came back to Sacramento," Tess explained, "which is where most of us in the Woods family lived then, he returned as a celebrated war hero. This photo here was taken on the day he received the Prisoner of War Medal for his valor and endurance."

Impressive.

"Not only that," Tess added, bragging further on his behalf, "your father was promoted to sergeant major after his release."

At the time I had no clue what that meant. But later I looked up the rank of sergeant major and learned that this was the highest rank enlisted soldiers could attain in the army. Uncle Dave, who was an army vet himself, told me that while every sergeant major is respected, those who have actually seen action are even more respected. "If your dad was a prisoner of war," Uncle Dave assured me, "he was at the top of the food chain when it comes to war heroes."

"How did my father die?" I asked Tess.

"He had complications in heart surgery," she answered. "He was only fifty years old when he died."

"He died young," Ma said.

"Do you have any other questions?" Tess asked.

"No," I said. But really, I did.

There were all sorts of questions exploding like fireworks inside my head. *How did my ma and dad meet? Were they ever married? Why did he leave us? Did Ma beat him up too, as she did Paul? What was he really like? Do you think he would have liked me?*

But I didn't dare ask any of these questions that were burning in my twelve-year-old soul. While I suspected Tess would know the answers, I sensed that this entire conversation had opened a gaping wound in my ma.

Since we'd arrived, Ma had been smoking cigarette after cigarette. If she'd played poker, fast smoking would have been her tell. Ma had grown increasingly agitated as the conversation progressed. All this talk about her past and about my birth had made her twitchy, so I just backed off.

After a few more minutes of small talk, we all said goodbye. I glanced over at the kid in the corner. I said goodbye to him, but he didn't notice—he was still spinning the stick with both hands, erupting periodically in joyful laughter.

Ma and I got in the car and drove back toward our apartment. Ma turned on the oldies station and chain-smoked. Rolling down the passenger side window, I peered out into the night, processing what I'd just learned.

I suspected Ma was still hiding something. Something she didn't want me to know.

What was she so ashamed of? Would whatever the secret was be even harder to hear? Would it help me better understand my story? Or deepen my insecurities?

Learning that my father was a decorated war hero had made me proud. But there was still an important piece of the puzzle missing. It would take another conversation before I would start getting the real answers I was still longing for.

And those answers would be hard to hear.

CHAPTER 17

FILLING IN THE BLANKS

MA WAS SITTING AT THE KITCHEN TABLE, a wreath of smoke encircling her head. She shook the last cigarette from the pack and said, "Go down to the 7-Eleven and get me two packs of Benson and Hedges Gold 100s." Ma handed me a $5 bill and quickly jotted a note for the cashier in her beautiful, flowing cursive. As usual, the note said, "Dear 7-Eleven Guy, please allow my son to buy me two packs of cigarettes. Sincerely, Shirley Taylor."

"You can buy a candy bar for yourself," she added absentmindedly, "but bring back the change."

I knew the drill. I'd done this dozens of times before. Whenever I handed the note to the attendant, he or she would look me up and down suspiciously. Then I'd say, "Trust me, you don't want my ma to have to come down here. Just sell me the cigarettes."

And they always did. Not once had they refused.

While I loved the Hershey's candy bars, I hated the cigarettes. I hated the way they smelled and the way they made my clothes smell. I hated holding my breath when I walked through the kitchen where Ma always sat and smoked. I hated that they were slowly killing her.

And I hated the way I could gauge how upset Ma was about something by how many cigarettes she was smoking—and how fast she was smoking them. When things were bad, she could blaze through a pack in no time flat.

On this particular day, she'd been smoking like a furnace. She was upset, and I knew why. In fact, *I* was the reason why. My very existence was the reason why she was upset—at least that's what my twelve-year-old head and heart told me. For the past couple of months, ever since the day Ma had first told me about my biological father, I'd been poking and prodding Ma to tell me more about my dad.

But every time, she shut me down cold. "I don't wanna talk about it," she'd say, shame flooding her eyes before she quickly cast them down, unable to meet my gaze.

Every boy wants to see his father as a hero of sorts, and Toney was that for sure. But just knowing that was not enough. I wanted details. I wanted to hear my ma unpack stories he had told of his escapades on the battlefield or his endurance as a POW in some back-jungle North Korean prison.

I was torn. On one hand, I was confused as to why he left my ma and me to begin with, but on the other hand, Toney had at least enough character to fight bravely on the battlefield and endure untold atrocities as a prisoner of war. Still, just knowing that was not enough for me. I wanted to know more. And I knew that Ma knew more.

Why does she shut me down cold every time I bring it up?

Ma was struggling financially (again), so we'd recently moved in with Grandpa and Grandma (again), who now lived north of Denver in Westminster. Ma lived upstairs, and I lived downstairs in their large unfinished basement.

Since the move, I was no longer a latchkey kid because Grandma was always home. Between Grandpa, Grandma, and Ma, I was the safest kid in the city. Although it really didn't matter that much anymore, since I was now living in a regular-size house in the safety of the suburbs.

Still, I felt unsettled—mostly because I was still processing the news about my biological father. I'd known about him for a couple of months now, and the more I thought about him, the more I wanted to know. If Ma wouldn't tell me more, I'd have to find out more some other way.

Maybe Grandma would know something about him. Since she was a natural-born storyteller, if I could just get her alone and get her talking, it was possible she would tell me more.

It wasn't long before I got my chance.

Grandma was cutting up vegetables for dinner when I walked into the kitchen looking for an after-school snack. As I cut myself a generous piece of apple pie, I was still considering how best to bring up the subject of my dad. But before I could muster my courage, Grandma surprised me by initiating the topic herself. "Greg, I never really heard how your meeting with Tess went awhile back. Tell me about it."

"Well," I said, "I found out that my dad was a war hero and all, but not much more than that."

"Did Tess or Shirley tell you how Toney and your ma met?" Grandma asked.

"Nope."

Turning from the cutting board, knife still in hand, she nodded toward the kitchen table and said, "Let's have a seat over there and I'll fill in some of the blanks for you."

"Okay, Grandma," I said, eagerly grabbing my pie and the glass of milk I'd poured. I could hardly believe my good luck.

"Before I tell you this, I need you to swear that you'll never tell your mama what I'm about to tell you," she whispered in a low voice, her steely eyes piercing into me.

"I swear, Grandma," I promised. "I won't say a thing."

"Tess was Shirley's friend and Toney's sister-in-law, and she played matchmaker," Grandma began. "They partied, and your mother got pregnant."

"What did he do when he found out?" I asked.

"He got himself transferred to Atlanta or something. I guess he was pretty high up in the army, so he had a lot of pull," Grandma said.

"He was a sergeant major," I said proudly.

"Well, sergeant major or not, he skipped town because he didn't want to be responsible for a kid," Grandma lamented. "That's what I'm guessin', anyway."

"So what did Ma do?" I asked.

"For several months, she kept her pregnancy a secret from us," Grandma admitted.

"Why?" I asked.

"Guess she was ashamed," Grandma said.

"Ma lived a pretty wild life, didn't she, Grandma?" I asked, already knowing the answer.

"Yeah," she affirmed. "From the time she was a teenager, we just couldn't get a handle on her. She used to leave the house in the middle of the night and go who knows where. And she had such a hair-trigger temper—just like Jack. We didn't really know how to deal with her. The stricter Grandpa got with her, the more she rebelled. So after a while, we just let her be. There was no stoppin' her. She's got Mathias blood.

"Anyway, back to the story. So one day, she tells us out of the blue that she's gonna take Doug on a trip to Boston to visit your Uncle Tommy and Aunt Carol. And she just packed up, got in the car, and left with Doug. He was around seven years old at the time."

Grandma paused and got a far-off look in her eyes as she remembered back across the years.

"I didn't find out until months later that she'd actually driven to Atlanta to try to find Toney and beg him to make her baby legitimate. She didn't want to have a child out of wedlock and disappoint me and your grandpa again. I just wish she would have told us."

"Why didn't she, do you think?" I asked.

"Your ma may act tough, but she's really soft underneath. She always felt like she fell short of what your grandpa and I wanted for her—and she did. Your ma was raised going to Bethany Baptist Church, but she never could see past the list of dos and don'ts to the love that God really has for her."

As Grandma was talking, I knew deep down that this was true. Ma thought Christianity was about cleaning up your life so God would let you into heaven. She just didn't get it that

God loved her no matter what she did or didn't do. It was starting to click now why she thought of herself as a bum and why across all those years that we'd lived in small apartments with thin walls, I had often heard her crying herself to sleep.

"She called your Uncle Tommy and Aunt Carol and told them her situation," Grandma continued. "Your ma told them she was pregnant and that the guy wanted nothing to do with her. She was at the end of her rope. She told Carol she didn't think she was going to keep the baby. She said she couldn't afford another kid."

Grandma was so caught up in her story, it was almost like she was oblivious to the fact that the baby she was talking about Ma aborting was me. But *I* wasn't oblivious. This felt like a bombshell had blown up in my face.

"Carol, being a blunt former Catholic from Boston, told her to come stay with them and they'd figure it out. That was Carol's way of stalling so that she could talk her out of an abortion," Grandma said.

"When Tommy was young, he was in the navy reserves but got called up to active duty during the Korean War. He was one of the cooks on a minesweeping ship. He was the calmest and steadiest of all our kids. Not that he was a wimp—he got into bodybuilding as a teenager, which burned off a lot of energy for him. He won second place for Mr. Colorado and several other bodybuilder awards. When he went off to the navy, he avoided a lot of the trouble that your other uncles got caught up in. He just always had a calmer way about him."

Grandma continued, "Tommy met Carol during his two-year stint in the navy. Eventually they got married. That's when your mother contacted them from Georgia, where she had been looking for your biological father—without any luck. Of course, all the while she was keeping this whole mess a secret from me and your grandfather.

"Out of all our kids, Tommy was the one who really stuck with church. After his two-year hitch with the navy, he eventually landed a good job just outside of Boston. Both he and Carol got involved with the local Baptist church," Grandma explained.

Pulling Grandma back to the story I actually cared about, I asked, "Why did Ma want to abort me anyway?"

"It wasn't really you she wanted to abort. It was her shame. She felt guilty from the time she was a teenager and started rebelling, and it has just gotten worse over the years," Grandma explained. "To make matters worse, this was all before *Roe v. Wade* made abortion legal, so your ma was trying to get as far away as possible from us and figure out some way to get it done."

"So what happened?" I asked in a quiet voice, still stunned by the news that I had been so unwanted that my ma had thought seriously about killing me. *It seems my series of close brushes with death started before I was even born.*

"Your ma and Doug moved in with Tommy and Carol for six months. During those months, Tommy and Carol kept encouraging her to have the baby and talked her into going to church with them a few times. But she felt as comfortable in church as a cow at the butcher shop."

"How did you and Grandpa find out about all this?" I wondered out loud.

"Tommy and Carol eventually convinced your ma to call us, and she finally did. She was a mess," Grandma confided. "But we told her to come back and have the baby here—to have *you*." Grandma paused to look directly at me and smile. "She left her car with Tommy and Carol as a kind of six-months'-rent payment and bought two bus tickets. She was eight months pregnant by the time she got back home to Denver."

"I guess you guys all saved my life 'cause you talked Ma out of aborting me," I said, finally ready to express my hurt aloud to Grandma.

Patting me on the hand, Grandma said, "I guess we did." Tears welled up in her eyes.

Seeing Grandma's sadness triggered a new emotion inside me. My own hurt over this unfolding story abruptly shifted to anger, like a sudden storm blowing in after a calm sea. "Why in the world would my father abandon my ma?" I demanded.

"I don't know, Greg. I don't know much about Toney other than what I just told you. I just know that he broke your ma's heart and that he didn't want to have anything to do with being your father."

The more I thought about it, the madder I got. *How dare this guy have sex with my ma and then skip town because he didn't want to live with the consequences!*

I pictured my ma driving from Denver to Atlanta, trying to figure out where Toney was stationed. I imagined her driving through the night with tears in her eyes and fears in her heart. She could barely afford taking care of herself, let alone two boys. And she did it all without child support or government assistance.

Something I'd never felt before started to well up in my heart: hate.

I hate Toney. I hate him for abandoning me. I hate him even more for abandoning my ma. He's the reason she cries herself to sleep at night.

Ma lost not only love, but also hope.

If Tess had lied to me about him being dead and he was still alive, I would kill him. I knew where my grandparents kept their guns. Heck, they taught me how to shoot to kill someone when I was five years old.

"Grandma," I said, looking straight at her, "I hate my dad, but I love my ma. And I'm not going to let her die a bitter, broken woman. Doug and me and Uncle Jack and Uncle Bob, we've all been trying to lead her to Christ for years. We've invited her to church. We've tried to turn conversations toward Jesus over and over. But Ma just shuts all of us down before we hardly get started by saying stuff like 'I'm too much of a bum for God to forgive me' and 'You don't know the things I've done wrong. God could never forgive me.'"

But now I did know.

Maybe this will help me reach her, I thought. While I promised Grandma I would never mention this story to Ma, I thought maybe knowing this would help me explain the gospel to her in a way she would connect with.

"Greg," Grandma said, interrupting my thoughts, "I've been praying for that for years. I will pray God gives you the right words to say."

But the right words are sometimes tough to come by. I wondered if I had it in me to find them.

CHAPTER 18

TIMBER!

THE LOUD BUZZ OF THE SCHOOL BELL interrupted my dark thoughts. I'd been stewing in the bile of bitterness toward my biological father all day. To me, he was not my dad—he was a sperm donor. To me, he wasn't a war hero—he was a deserter. He abandoned my ma after she'd gotten pregnant and ran away like a coward. Every time I thought about it, an anger I didn't know I was capable of, a Mathias-level fury, would turn my face beet red, raise my pulse rate beyond the safety zone, and fill the veins in my neck with red-hot rage. His abandonment of my ma infuriated me. I hated him.

But I'd grown adept at compartmentalizing my hatred for my dad away from the rest of my "kind and loving, good Christian boy" life, so I quickly shut down my dark thoughts, ready to move on to the next exciting thing.

Even though the school bell marked the end of the day, most of us students weren't actually headed home. Instead, we milled around outside the front of the school next to the line of waiting school buses. Once one of the teachers signaled it was time to board, we packed into the yellow buses like sardines in a can for the ride down to the Denver Coliseum to attend *The Basic Seminar*—or as our teachers called it, "The Bill Gothard Seminar."

While attendance at the seminar wasn't a school requirement, it was "strongly encouraged" by our teachers. "Strongly encouraged" was their way of saying, "If you want to stay on our good side, you should really try to be there." That's why most of the kids were going.

I sat next to my new friend, Rick Long, during the noisy, bumpy thirty-minute ride. Rick had started at Arvada Christian School just a few months earlier, at the beginning of the school year. Even though I was a freshman and he was a seventh grader, I saw something special in him. He was more serious about loving the Lord and reaching the lost than a lot of the kids at school.

Although Rick was raised in the suburbs and I was raised in the highest crime-rate area of Denver, the Long family had a gospel grittiness about them that attracted me. His parents ran a halfway house for wayward girls, and over the years, as they shared the love of Jesus with them, they had led many of them to Christ. Rick had learned from his parents' example what it meant to have a passion for God and compassion for the hurting.

"Do you know what this seminar is actually about?" Rick asked.

"Some kind of training to help us spiritually," I answered.

Attending extracurricular events like this wasn't drudgery for me. I'd seen how the power of the gospel had been transforming my family one by one, and I wanted to be the best witness for Christ I could possibly be. There were still two lost souls in my family I desperately wanted to reach—my still-too-guilty-for-Jesus ma, who I had been consistently trying to share the gospel with, and my out-of-state Uncle Richard. My other uncles had repeatedly tried to share the gospel with him over the phone, but he shut them down every time.

Maybe I'd discover some keys to getting the conversation going with Richard and breaking through to my ma. Plus, I'd heard the buzz about how transformational this seminar was for many of our teachers who had previously experienced it. It was supposedly a game changer, and I wanted to be changed.

Mr. Gothard had been an icon in the fundamentalist, home school, and Christian school underground for decades. Over the years, millions had attended his events. He routinely packed arenas, coliseums, and auditoriums across the nation with thousands of young people, filling young minds with his 1-2-3 easy brand of simple-answers fundamentalism.

Once our line of buses pulled into the Denver Coliseum parking lot, Rick and I parted ways. In strict, regimented order, all of us sorted ourselves into our class groupings and lined up alphabetically.

Even though I wanted to sit next to Rick, I realized it was probably a good thing we were divided into our class years. Rick and I were both full of adrenaline and jokes, which would have made us like nitro and glycerin in a conference setting. We loved the Lord, but we loved to joke around, too.

Once assembled in alphabetical lines, we marched to the

arena for check-in. Along with thousands of other young people, we received a large red book called *Institute in Basic Youth Conflicts*. The King James Bible may have been our official divinely inspired playbook, but this giant red book would soon become our unofficial pretribulational, premillennial, all-things-fundamental rule book.

The excitement was palpable as we made our way down the steep gray concrete stairs of the Denver Coliseum to find our seats. Thousands of young people filled the packed room. I sat down between Stephanie and Shawna, two of my fellow very-serious-for-the-Lord classmates whose last names bookended mine alphabetically.

The crowd hushed and the conference started, but to my surprise, the famous Mr. Gothard wasn't actually present to speak. Instead, a prerecorded video of him appeared on a big screen at the front of the hall as his voice boomed from the giant speakers on the stage.

"Seriously?" I said, turning to Shawna. "We're watching a video?"

In reality, I guess I shouldn't have been surprised. After all, this was no rock concert. We were fundamentalists, and fundies had no rhythm. My music teacher, Miss Widgren, had quoted Mr. Gothard in music class just a few weeks ago. "There's 'edifying music' and 'non-edifying music,'" she'd explained. "If you take a plant and expose it to classical music, it will grow. If you take a plant and expose it to rock 'n' roll music, it will die. Music is not amoral. The music itself is either spiritual or unspiritual. That's why you can't mix Christian lyrics and a rock 'n' roll beat. Some musical beats are from the devil, and some are from the Lord. The ones from the devil go against the natural beat of your heart." Her implication was that it was somehow physically dangerous to listen to rock music.

Even as a freshman, this seemed kind of stupid to me. Shooting my hand up in class, I'd said, "Well, if you time it right, Miss Widgren, it could be like heart aerobics." Everyone erupted in laughter—except Miss Widgren. Narrowing her eyes, she'd looked at me and said, "Greg, I need to talk to you after class." Since I'd developed a reputation as the "spiritual leader of the class," a ripple of "ewwws" and "uh-ohs" spread around the room.

That episode in music class had actually made me a little suspicious of where this whole seminar was going to go. Adding to my own skepticism about Bill Gothard's take on rock 'n' roll was an encounter I'd had with one of the new leaders at Youth Ranch, Mark Schweitzer. Mark and his wife, Kim, had come from the Youth Ranch movement's mother ship, Florida Bible College, just six months earlier. He had a whole different take on Christian music and, in a way, on what it meant to live a Christian life. Mark was a kind of "grace dealer" in the midst of Arvada Christian School's rule-heavy approach to the Christian faith.

Mark had taken me under his wing and was helping me to grow spiritually. As a fatherless teen, I was eager to have an older Christian male invest in me and help me grow in my walk with Christ, so I respected Mark and carefully considered everything he shared with me. Mark's views on "non-edifying" Christian music diverged dramatically from Mr. Gothard's. Mark avidly listened to all sorts of Christian rock, back in the fledgling days of the Christian music industry. He'd secretly introduced me to groups like Petra and DeGarmo and Key and to singers like

Dallas Holm, Wayne Watson, and Randy Stonehill. He even sneaked me into a David Meece concert once to give me an up-close-and-personal view of the burgeoning Christian music scene of the early '80s. I fell in love with Christian rock from that moment on.

"Don't tell Yankee that I took you to this concert," he warned, "or I'll get fired." It had all felt deliciously rebellious to me without actually being sinful.

Maybe it was because I'd seen so much "real sin" growing up that this didn't seem so bad. I'd witnessed more violence as a kid than most adults ever see in a lifetime. I'd seen heads and cars bashed in with baseball bats. I'd seen battle scars from countless street fights fueled by unbridled rage. I'd seen the devastating guilt that plagued my ma over a life of sexual immorality and being within a hair's breadth of having me murdered in her womb.

Listening to God-honoring words set to a rock-n-roll beat just didn't seem all that spiritually dangerous to me. When I listened to the songs Mark introduced me to, it didn't make me feel like sinning against God, it made me feel like serving him all the more. Watching Mark's life seemed proof enough for me that you could jam out with Christian music and live a life for God. And, contrary to what Miss Widgren said, his heart seemed to be beating just fine.

"What matters most," Mark had told me, "is that you focus on your relationship with God, not all the rules around this place. The rules can't make you holy. Just trust the Lord, keep your eyes on him, and refuse to allow a list of dos and don'ts to define you. Watch out for legalism."

I wasn't sure what legalism was, but Mark's warning echoed

in my head as Mr. Gothard's opening words filled the Denver Coliseum.

Still, as the evening progressed, I found that the middle-aged Mr. Gothard had a pleasant way about him. Up there on the big screen, his crisp suit matched his slicked-back, jet-black hair. He'd mastered a very direct yet still very pastoral way of teaching. He sprinkled his talk with Scripture, stories, and lots and lots of graphs. He spoke with authority without sounding like an authoritarian. Unlike Yankee, Jack Hyles, Curtis Hudson, and the other fundamentalist preachers I'd been weaned on, Bill Gothard had a more gentle way about him that drew me and the rest of the crowd in to hang on his every word.

But the real attraction of the seminar for me was not Bill Gothard; it was the content he developed and put into the giant red textbooks thousands of us were holding in our hands. It seemed like this book had all the answers to life. It was that big. As I flipped through it, I saw session titles like "6 Basic Steps to Conquer Impurity" and "7 Steps of Action When Asked to Do Something You Think Is Wrong" or "5 Basic Steps toward Becoming a Whole Person."

The simplicity of this approach appealed to me. Growing up in my wild family, much of my life had been a swirl of confusion, fear, longing, and searching. But this man and his giant red book seemed to have all the secrets, keys, and 1-2-3s.

My hand ached from all the note-taking. And I wasn't alone. If you listened closely during each of Bill Gothard's hour-and-twenty-minute talks, you could hear the scratching sound of pens meeting paper across the arena and, soon after, the simultaneous turning of numbered pages in our giant red handbooks for life.

Night after night that week, we came back. Night after night, I took copious notes. Night after night, Rick and I would talk about all we'd learned on the bus ride home. My head hurt from all the thoughts being crammed into my curious mind.

Gothard spoke with gentle authority on issues teens were interested in, including dating and "how far is too far" when it came to physical intimacy while dating. He also talked a lot about marriage, although he himself was single.

During one session I was challenged to begin thinking about and jotting down the attributes I wanted in a wife someday. I listed twenty-seven, and my list included "soul winner" twice. During another session, I learned about "the umbrella of authority" that everyone was under, especially wives and children.

I'd previously thought that living a Christian life was complicated, but while I was in the seminar eagerly listening to Bill Gothard's every word, it seemed, well, simple and easy. All I had to do was apply the list, walk through the 1-2-3s, and everything would turn out just fine.

Once a session or so, he would say something in passing that would give me pause—something that sounded like the laundry list of dos and don'ts that Mark had warned me about. But soon, Mr. Gothard would be on to some other truth or graph or insight that would convict and convince me.

Then Thursday night rolled around and changed my life forever.

The evening started like every other night. Mr. Gothard gave some opening remarks and prayed. Then he dived into the topic for the evening—letting go of bitterness and choosing to forgive those who have wronged you.

I squirmed in my seat uncomfortably.

Working through another one of his 1-2-3 lists, Bill Gothard sounded like he was speaking directly to me and me alone. He was describing the depth of my bitterness and hatred toward my father like I was an open book.

"There's a third reason that we can't afford to be bitter," he said, "and that is because we become like the one we're bitter toward. One day a high school girl said to me in just real bitterness, 'I hate my aunt.' And I said, rather casually, 'That's too bad.' She said, 'Why'd you say it that way for?' I said, 'Within twenty years, you're gonna be just like your aunt.' She said, 'Oh, no, oh horrors! I'll forgive her then!'"

Mr. Gothard's message was cutting deep. Like a lumberjack chopping down a large tree, he was relentless, and so was the Holy Spirit. Again and again, he swung his axe of spiritual truth.

"When you hate someone," he explained, taking his first swing at me, "that person becomes the object of your 'emotional focus.'" Using the example of a bad dad, he said, "When a son hates his father because the father was a drunk or unfaithful or whatever, even though the son may never become a drunk or unfaithful or whatever, he will begin to adopt the same 'root attitudes' that drive the father's external behavior. Sons who are emotionally riveted to their father's external sins will soon adopt the same underlying attitudes of pride, bitterness, or selfishness as their fathers. Years later, people will approach the sons and say, 'You are just like your father,' not because of the same external conduct, but because of the same root attitudes."

The axe blow hit home. In my estimation, Toney was a drunk and a philanderer and everything I didn't want to be as a man. But would I become just like him? Was this hatred in my heart going to conform me to his image?

I wasn't ready to surrender yet. I clenched my fist and tightened my throat and waited for the conviction that had landed its first blow to pass. I hoped Gothard would change the illustration to forgiving a spouse or change the topic to dating or anything other than this "forgive your father" talk.

I stood my ground and fought hard not to give in.

But then he swung his axe again. "If God can forgive us for all the sins we've committed against him, then you can forgive anyone for any sins they may have committed against you."

With another swing, he described in vivid detail how carrying bitterness could impact me physically, emotionally, and spiritually.

Then with another swing, he talked about the futility of being offended on behalf of someone else, like I was for my abandoned mother.

With every point he made, every graph he drew, and every Scripture he quoted, wood chips flew.

Then with one mighty, last swing he told the story of the unforgiving servant from Matthew 18:23-35:

> The kingdom of heaven is like a king who wanted
> to settle accounts with his servants. As he began the
> settlement, a man who owed him ten thousand bags
> of gold was brought to him. Since he was not able to
> pay, the master ordered that he and his wife and his
> children and all that he had be sold to repay the debt.
>
> At this the servant fell on his knees before him.
> "Be patient with me," he begged, "and I will pay back

everything." The servant's master took pity on him, canceled the debt and let him go.

But when that servant went out, he found one of his fellow servants who owed him a hundred silver coins. He grabbed him and began to choke him. "Pay back what you owe me!" he demanded.

His fellow servant fell to his knees and begged him, "Be patient with me, and I will pay it back."

But he refused. Instead, he went off and had the man thrown into prison until he could pay the debt. When the other servants saw what had happened, they were outraged and went and told their master everything that had happened.

Then the master called the servant in. "You wicked servant," he said, "I canceled all that debt of yours because you begged me to. Shouldn't you have had mercy on your fellow servant just as I had on you?" In anger his master handed him over to the jailers to be tortured, until he should pay back all he owed.

This is how my heavenly Father will treat each of you unless you forgive your brother or sister from your heart.

My last defenses fell.

I was the unforgiving servant. My master had forgiven me my great debt of sin. Jesus hung on a cross made of wood, saying, "Father, forgive them; they don't know what they are doing." He was the only innocent one, and he forgave those who sinned against him. He forgave *me*.

In that moment, the pen I had been taking notes with was

no longer a writing instrument; it was the axe blade, chopping away at my stubborn heart. It was my sin that had nailed Jesus to the cross. The crimson red of my textbook reminded me of his blood poured out for me.

If Jesus could forgive me, then I could forgive anyone—even Toney.

But Mr. Gothard interrupted my thoughts again. "Let's bow for prayer. It is so important that we conquer bitterness. I wonder if, just now, each one couldn't think of those individuals who have offended us, wronged us, damaged us . . . would you right now be able to say, 'God, you've forgiven me of so much, would you also forgive me now for having a temporal value system? Would you forgive me for an unloving spirit toward those who have offended me? . . . Right now, I do fully forgive those who offended me.' Would you tell that to God and really mean it? 'I fully release them.'"

God, will you forgive me?

Then something happened that I wasn't expecting. I began to cry. Not just cry, but weep. Not just weep, but wail.

The moment had so overwhelmed me that for those several seconds, I was completely unaware that my crying was so loud and so obvious that my fellow students around me were reacting—some with whispering, most with giggling, and a few with sympathy. But my sole business in that moment was forgiveness, and with all the strength I had, I choked out the words that I'd resisted for so long. "Dad, I forgive you."

Timber!

For the first time in my life, the chasm that had been created in my soul in the absence of an earthly father was flooded by the love of my heavenly Father. With every hot, salty tear that flowed down my cheeks and landed on the cold Coliseum concrete beneath my seat, I sensed the love of God flooding on me, in me, and over me.

God was my dad, and he would never leave me or forsake me. It didn't matter whose physical DNA I carried. I was neither bodybuilder nor war hero; I was a child of my Papa in paradise, the King of the universe, God himself. Nothing else mattered to me in that life-defining moment.

After the seminar dismissed, I took my seat next to Rick on the bus. "What did you think of tonight's session?" he asked me.

"I forgave my dad for the first time," I said simply.

Not understanding the full impact of my statement, he said, "That's cool!"

It *was* cool. But forgiving my father was just a start. There was someone else in my life who desperately needed to experience forgiveness. Not mine, but God's.

CHAPTER 19

"CIGARETTES AND ALL"

FOUR YEARS EARLIER, when I was eleven, I had begged and begged Ma to send me to Arvada Christian School, the small, private school Yankee and his crew were launching. I'd desperately wanted to be one of the original nineteen students when it first opened—not nineteen in my class, but nineteen in the entire school!

I begged Ma to send me to ACS. But Ma's raw, unvarnished answer was "There's no way in hell that I can afford to send you to a Christian school! We barely have enough money for food! I'm behind on my bills, and there's no way I'm taking government assistance!"

Down deep inside I knew it was true. She couldn't afford it. *We* couldn't afford it. Standing there, my mind drifted back to a few years earlier in our old dingy apartment in North Denver. Ma was so desperate for cash that one day she reluctantly walked into my room and, with her head low, said, "Greg, I have to ask you for a favor."

"What is it, Ma?" I asked.

"We're out of money for groceries, and I was wondering if I could borrow your fifty dollars' worth of pennies so that we can eat this week."

Over the years I had collected those pennies and stored them in a large glass jar that I kept in my closet. I collected them from sidewalks, from between couch cushions, and even from sewer grates. Every time I dropped my newly found pennies into that jar and watched it slowly fill to the top, I felt rich. Every time I heard the clink of them landing on the other pennies, I felt hope. To be honest, I didn't want to give them to her. I had worked hard to collect every last one of those pennies. But I knew that she felt bad for asking me, so I said, "Okay, Ma."

"I'll pay you back—I promise," she said.

Well, days turned to weeks and weeks turned to months. Every once in a while I'd ask, "Ma, are you gonna pay me back for those pennies?"

And she would say, "Yes. Trust me, I will. Just give me a little more time to get back on my feet."

I trusted her. I knew she'd pay me back eventually.

And now two years later, here was my chance to get paid back.

When Ma told me she couldn't afford to send me to Yankee's Christian school, I said, "Ma, remember that fifty dollars' worth of pennies you borrowed from me a few years back?"

She bowed her head once again and said, "Yes."

I said, "If you send me to that Christian school, you don't have to pay me back."

I'll never forget the determination in her eyes when she looked up at me. She said, "I'll send you to the Christian school."

Of course, it wasn't just my innocent bargaining chip that motivated her. She sensed I needed something more, something deeper. She knew I was still searching for my purpose, for my calling. And she hoped that Yankee's Christian school would help me figure out a direction for my life. So although she was not a Christian herself, she was bound and determined to help me become the best Christian I could be and to, hopefully, find my purpose in the process.

Although she thought herself unworthy of God's grace, she took a special pride in helping me thrive in my own faith. It wasn't quite penance for the sins of her past, but I sometimes wondered whether me going to a Christian school soothed her inflamed conscience, like aloe vera on a sunburn.

Over the four years I'd been at Arvada Christian, I was thriving in a way I never had in public school. At my old school, I'd been a scared, bullied kid. Now I was gaining in boldness and confidence. I'd been an average student in public school, but now my grades were all As. And after Timo's "Bound for Hell" assignment at the mall a few months back, a purpose was taking shape in the center of my soul, and that purpose was helping to bring positive change to every aspect of my life.

Ma saw the difference Arvada Christian was making in my life and was propelled to sacrifice for me and my future in order to pay the tuition. Ma worked double shifts. She held garage sales. She put some of her things up for cash at the nearby pawn shop when necessary.

Ever since I'd transferred schools, Ma had been hearing the gospel more and more often. Yankee would give the gospel at every school function. But she wasn't interested—not because she hated God, but because she was convinced God hated her for all her transgressions.

And since she was convinced that she was on a highway to hell, she chose to have a bit of fun from time to time by shocking the insular Christian school community with her bold, blunt, and brazen behavior.

The snarkier and more uptight my suburban classmates' parents were, the more she would try to unwind them. She loved making them cringe by seasoning her sentences with curse words like salt on a steak.

Most were patient. Some were offended. A few were aghast. Nobody was more shocked than Mrs. Carlson (not her real name). She was Colorado Bible Church's and Arvada Christian School's very own pointy-fingered, furrow-browed, hyperlegalistic church lady.

For the most part, I was able to keep my ma away from her at school functions. But sometimes that was impossible because her son and I were friends. Once when I asked my ma to drop me off at Mrs. Carlson's house, I sensed there might be trouble, so I asked her to stay in the car. But she insisted on walking me to the door.

"No," Ma said. "I want to see what time I'm supposed to pick you up." To my relief, she at least chose to put her cigarette out in the car's built-in ashtray, rather than puffing it all the way to the "God Bless All Who Enter Here"-signed door.

"Ma, don't say anything mean to Mrs. Carlson if she answers the door," I pleaded as we walked up the narrow sidewalk toward her house.

"I won't if she doesn't. I will if she does," Ma said, reminding me that she wouldn't take any guff from anyone, at any time, for any reason.

Mrs. Carlson opened the door with a half-crooked smile that quickly morphed into a frown as she peered more closely at my ma.

"Well, Shirley, you got your hair cut short. That's . . . *interesting*."

"Do you like it?" Ma asked, not getting the not-so-sanctified sarcasm. Ma leaned her head to the side and touched her hair the way a model would.

"No, I actually *don't* like it. I don't like it at all," Mrs. Carlson said, practically snarling.

My heart rate quickened because this was going bad quickly.

"Why the hell not?" Ma asked, her attempted suburban demeanor quickly morphing back to North Denver street tough.

"Because it's a sin for a woman to have short hair according to the Bible," Mrs. Carlson huffed.

"Why is it a sin?" Ma asked, part angry and part wondering.

"It's a sin because you look like a man," Mrs. Carlson said.

That was like throwing down an insult before a street fight. But instead of punching this lightweight in the throat with her fist, Ma knocked her out with words. Ma looked her up and down, leaned in, and said, "Honey, you could shave off all my hair, hang me upside down, and paint me green, and I'd still look more like a woman than you ever will."

With that she wheeled around and strutted back to her newly purchased but extremely used 1969 pearly white Chevrolet Impala. Mrs. Carlson almost passed out on the spot.

Needless to say, it was an awkward and quiet walk to my friend's room. But on the bright side, Ma was learning to use her words and not just her fists.

Still, even after four years of rubbing shoulders with other Christian parents, hearing the gospel at every school function, and listening to me subtly apply some of what I was learning about evangelism on her, Ma was no closer to coming to Christ. Being around more Christians probably made her feel more guilty. And being around judgmental Christians like Mrs. Carlson likely reinforced Ma's misperception that the gospel was about cleaning up your behavior to earn God's love. She knew she could never be good enough to earn her way into heaven. She saw herself as a sinner beyond redemption.

So after years of trying to be subtle about sharing Jesus with her, I became convinced that a new approach was necessary. Instead of beating around the bush or waiting until she was in the right mood, I was going to just do it the Mathias way—a straightforward gospel punch to the face.

On the chosen day for the big conversation, I waited nervously for Ma's return home from work. I paced back and forth in my basement room, praying for boldness and just the right words to say.

When I heard her come through the door upstairs, I could tell from the distinctive creaks in the floor above me that she had plopped down at the kitchen table, most likely to smoke a few after a long, hard day.

I knew I was prayed up and ready. It was time. I marched upstairs and into the kitchen with a boldness that surprised her and said, "Ma, I need to talk to you about something super important."

"What is it? Your grades? Did ya knock a girl up? Did ya kill somebody? What?" she asked with a teasing smile.

"No, Ma. I'm totally serious right now, so I need you to pay attention." I spoke with a seriousness she wasn't used to seeing—not since the day I'd grilled her about George Stier and had learned about Toney.

"Okay, I'm listening, Greg. What is it?"

I barreled ahead before I lost my nerve. "I don't want you to go to hell. Doug doesn't want you to go to hell. Grandma doesn't want you to go to hell. I'm sick and tired of you saying that you're too sinful or that I don't know the things you've done wrong. It doesn't matter, Ma. The Bible says, 'Today is the day of salvation.' Now is the time to believe!"

She paused for a moment, studying the seriousness of my face and the fierce focus of my eyes. Then she said, "Okay, Greg, explain it to me one more time, and I'll listen. I'll really listen."

So I sat down, leaned in, and said, "Ma, God loves you. He really, really loves you. He made you to be in fellowship with him. That's how he feels about all of humanity. John 3:16 starts with the words, 'For God so loved the world . . .'"

I could tell she was locked in, so I continued. "But the sins we commit separate us from him." I put my hand up in a halt gesture to stop her before she could tell me one more time how much of a sinner she was. "And it doesn't matter how big or small those sins are. If you sin once, you're out, which means we're all out!"

"Out of what?" Ma interrupted.

"We're out of relationship with him. We're out of luck. We're out of options. Because our sins cannot be removed by good deeds. Our good deeds just cover over our sin, like frosting on a burnt cake."

"I've burned plenty of cakes," Ma said with a smile.

I continued. "So, God sent his only Son, Jesus, into the world to live the perfect life we could never live and die in our place for our sins on the cross."

"But what about the really bad ones?" Ma asked, leaning in even farther.

"Every sin is really bad to God, and Jesus died in our place for all our sins on the cross. That's why some of his last words on the cross were 'It is finished,' because the price of our sin had been paid in full."

The term "paid in full" struck her. The payment for her sins wasn't on layaway. And her sins weren't up to her to pay anyway. Her guilt, her constant verbal self-flagellation, her working double shifts to send me to a Christian school, her late-night tears—none of it could wipe her sins or her shame away. Only Jesus could.

The light began to dawn.

I quoted the rest of the verse that I had started with. "For God so loved the world, that he gave his only begotten Son, that whosoever believeth in him should not perish, but have everlasting life."

"What the hell does that mean?" Ma asked with the utmost sincerity.

I laughed as I remembered that Ma—who had never finished high school—didn't speak King Jimmy. "It means that if you believe Jesus died in your place on the cross and rose again, and you trust in him alone to save you, then all your sins are forgiven, and he gives you the gift of eternal life."

Ma had one more question. "You mean to tell me that all that I have to do is to believe that Jesus died for all my sins, and bada boom, all my sins are forgiven just like that?" She snapped her fingers.

"Yeah, Ma, that's what the Bible says."

She leaned back, took a long drag on her cigarette, blew the smoke out sideways from her mouth, looked at me, and said, "Okay, I'm in."

And when my ma said she was in, she was in.

Right then I prayed with her, and I could sense her praying too. For the first time, she was talking to the one who loved her so much. For the first time, she was experiencing the unconditional love she had longed for all these years. For the first time, she realized that even a "bum" like her could be forgiven.

One of the things I learned at school was to always "quiz" someone after they've trusted in Jesus to make sure they've understood the message.

"So, Ma, where are you going to go when you die?" I asked.

"I'm going to heaven, cigarettes and all," she answered. We both laughed.

"Heaven's non-smoking, Ma," I cracked back. "But seriously, why are you going to heaven?"

She said, "Because Jesus died for all my sins, even the really bad ones."

Ma had crossed from death to life. And God had used *me* to reach her—me, her almost aborted son. I, the weak one in my family, had just been used by God to lead the strongest person I had ever met to Christ. This was a different kind of power than the pec-stretching, bench-pressing, bicep-flexing power of my uncles. This was divine power, resurrection power, power that turned sinners into saints, losers into loved ones, and bums into believers.

I lay in bed that night and reflected on the amazing events of the day. *If Ma can trust in Christ, then anyone can trust in Christ.*

I was so happy!

But my excitement was cut short. The grim reaper who had knocked so often at my door was about to kick in the door and snatch someone very close to me.

CHAPTER 20

PREACHER BOY

AFTER A RAPID-FIRE THREE KNOCKS, Mr. Newhard, the math teacher everyone was afraid of, pushed open the door of Miss Chester's biology class. We'd nicknamed this short, slender, super-serious teacher "the Warden" because he was a by-the-book kind of teacher who was short on mercy and high on compliance. The Warden scanned the room until his intense gaze fell on me.

His piercing eyes stared at me through the thick lenses of his George McFly–style horn-rimmed glasses for a few uncomfortable moments. "Greg," he announced sternly in his monotone voice, "Pastor Arnold wants you in his office right away."

My heart dropped. Pastor Arnold (aka Yankee) was large and in charge, at least from my fifteen-year-old sophomore vantage point. To be called into his office was a big deal—and usually not a good deal.

"Okay," I said hesitantly. A murmur of distress rippled around the room but was quickly silenced by one of the Warden's raised eyebrows.

As I death-marched down the hallway toward Yankee's office, I breathed deeply, trying to calm my pounding heart. But the smell wafting down the hallway—an unpleasant mix of sweaty teenagers, Jean Naté After Bath Splash, and Brut cologne—was anything but calming.

My mind scrolled through the last few weeks trying to recollect anything I'd done that was bad enough to get me summoned to the one office everyone tried to avoid. Maybe it had something to do with me being the class clown. In my old neighborhood, I was the wimpy white kid who used to run home from school to escape the bullies. I was the weak boy the uncles whispered about, questioning my manhood. But here at my small Christian school in the suburbs, I'd gained a reputation as a funny man.

I'd started cracking jokes out loud during my junior high years. At family gatherings, I could never get a word in edgewise, so I never tried. But as I'd listened to my family's jokes and stories across the years, I'd learned something about the art of cracking jokes and telling engaging, hilarious stories. There had been times I'd gotten my fellow students laughing so hard, the teacher had lost control of the class.

Or maybe one of my recent pranks had landed me in hot water. Had the Warden found out that a group of friends and I had recently TPed his house? Was it that my buddy Rick and I had dressed like women in a recent youth group skit, somehow violating the Fundamentalists' Conduct Code of No Cross-Dressing? Or maybe Pastor Arnold had heard that my friend Art and I had snuck into Arvada West High School and put gospel tracts in every single school locker, being careful to evade the custodian roaming the halls.

Compared to my family's crimes in years past, these seemed like baby sins to me. But in legalistic settings, baby sins grow fat on judgment milk.

Still, I took some comfort in the fact that Yankee liked me. After all, besides being the class clown, I was also hardworking and studious. When I started attending Arvada Christian, my grandfather said, "I'll give you a dollar for every A you get at school." As a result, one of my biggest joys was watching Grandpa scan my report card every semester and give me a crisp $1 bill for every A. It wasn't the money I cared about as much as what that money represented—Grandpa's approval. Since Grandpa was the gold standard of manhood to me, his approval meant the world.

Another reason Yankee liked me was that I was one of his aspiring "preacher boys."

"Preacher boy" was the title independent fundamentalist pastors gave to their handpicked, up-and-coming preachers-in-waiting. To have that title was a big deal, and I had sought with all my heart to earn that accolade.

Once a year, Christian school attendees from all over Colorado gathered together for speech and music contests that would range from dramatic readings to singing solos (think a fundamentalist's version of *The Voice*, minus music with any heart-out-of-sync-ing, sin-inducing rock 'n' roll beat), to choir competitions, to the granddaddy of them all: the contest to see who would be the next great young preacher.

It was a fundamentalist's showcase of the young, straitlaced, and talented. Whichever Christian school came out on top with the most winners would wear the honor like a badge for the next twelve months and use it to recruit more prospective preachers for their school.

Silver State Baptist School was the big kahuna in the competition. They had more students, more money, and more talent.

But we had more grit. Although Arvada Christian was not even close to being among the bigger schools competing, we seemed to always be fighting with Silver State for more trophies, more ribbons, more medals.

Yankee and his crew of young teachers—many of whom he had personally won to Christ and discipled—gave 100 percent and expected 100 percent. Yankee had a genuine zeal to win souls and produce soul winners. Even the term *soul winner*—an old-school term for Christians who share the gospel with the intent of "winning" lost souls for Christ—sounded like a competition. It sounded like it because it was. At Arvada Christian, pretty much everything was a competition—from how many verses you could memorize, to how many times you could read through the Bible, to how many souls you could win to Christ.

So it was only natural that preaching had been turned into a competition too. Everyone wanted to see who was going to be the next great young preacher. The first sermon I ever preached was during one of these statewide preaching competitions.

Preaching out of Colossians 1:28-29, I'd literally shaken with terror throughout my ten-minute sermon as I'd attempted to paint a clear picture of the discipline it takes to preach the gospel in a way that we may "present every man perfect in Christ Jesus." Even though I was stricken with a toxic combo of stage fright and fear of failure, those feelings somehow morphed into frenetic energy as I preached. By the time I was finished, the fear boiling in my soul was equal parts panic and passion.

When the judges' evaluations came back, their score sheets noted my "great intensity" and "amazing passion." One even noted that I'd literally shaken the pulpit with my preaching zeal. But what the judge mistook for preaching power I knew was a cocktail of terror, truth, and triumph. Still, I'd finally found something I was good at.

After that first event, I'd entered every preaching competition I could. Once, Yankee had even let me preach a ten-minute sermon in big church to showcase one of his up-and-coming preacher boys to the adults.

The accolades were like an addictive drug to me. Unlike my uncles and cousins, I didn't have the physical frame to be a bodybuilder. I didn't have the anger to be a fighter. And I didn't have the coordination to be an athlete.

But I had the same adrenaline-laced DNA in my body as my uncles and ma. This twitchy DNA had triggered countless back-alley brawls in the old neighborhood when it came to my family. Their particular strand of DNA stood for "Do Not Annoy"—or you'll be desperately sorry. But for me, DNA more appropriately stood for my "Dread of Non-Acceptance." Having struggled all my life with feeling like a misfit in my own family, I had a burning desire for both peer acceptance and adult approval coursing through my veins. That was one of the underlying drives behind my constant jokes, my obsessive study habits, and my desire to be an award-winning preacher and spiritual leader. When it came to bodybuilding, I was a nobody, but when it came to flexing my comedic, scholastic, and spiritual leadership biceps, I could pose with the best of them.

This odd combo of class clown, star pupil, and potential preacher boy was frequently baffling to my teachers, but it was working well for me. My jokes got me accepted into various friend groups. My studies satisfied the quiet curiosity about life, God, and everything that I'd had since I was a kid. And preaching gave me a way to express my burning urgency to reach the lost and to help others see the "Bound for Hell" sign that Timo had helped me to see that night at the mall.

But it wasn't just urgency that lit up my preaching. It was surety—the surety that the gospel could change lives (as it had changed mine), change families (as it was changing mine), and change entire cities (as was happening through Youth Ranch in our city and cities across the nation, especially in South Florida).

Maybe being one of Yankee's beloved "preacher boys" would buy me some favor to counteract any transgression I had committed over the last week or two.

All this was swirling around in my mind as I made the long walk down the hallway to Yankee's office. Mr. Newhard was watching me from the door of the classroom every step of the way. I could feel his eyes burning a hole through my back like a laser of judgment made stronger by the thick lenses in his glasses.

When I knocked on Yankee's half-open door, he looked up from his papers and said, "Hello, Greg, please take a seat."

As strict as Yankee was as our pastor, he was usually very congenial. He was quick with a warm smile and a corny joke to put others at ease, especially students. But there was no smile and no joke as he got up and shut the door behind me.

He took his seat and looked across his big desk at me, pausing to consider how to say what he was about to say. Then he just said it. "Greg, I have some bad news for you. Your grandfather has suffered a massive heart attack and is at the hospital. They don't think he's going to make it."

After hearing those words, my audio comprehension froze up. Yankee kept talking. I could see his mouth moving and hear sounds coming out of his mouth, but nothing further registered. I was in complete and utter shock.

Grandpa is dying. The strong one, the freakishly strong one, the closest person I've ever had to a dad, is struggling for every breath in a hospital bed.

I didn't cry. I just sat there in shock.

CHAPTER 21

"YOU AIN'T GETTIN' ME, BOY!"

MA WALKED INTO THE SCHOOL OFFICE without checking in with the school secretary—who knew better than to try to stop her—and wrapped me in a big hug. There were tear streaks down her cheeks, and her eyes were red and puffy. We drove in silence to St. Anthony North Hospital, where the ambulance had taken Grandpa.

As Ma and I entered his room, I was taken aback by what I saw. My short, stocky grandpa who filled the bed with his girth lay there still and silent. Whenever his eyelids opened briefly, his eyes rolled up and down, then back and forth, in their sockets.

Grandma and Ma fell into each other's arms and cried.

Over the next few hours, my uncles and aunts began to fill his room, shedding tears and sobbing intermittently in sudden bursts of loud Mathias grief. My family had big muscles and big emotions. They hit hard, laughed hard, and cried hard.

And they were hit hard by this. The strongest man we had ever known had been laid low by the death that was slowly encasing him like a shroud, waiting for his last breath to escape.

I still had not shed one tear, and I felt bad about it.

Why can't I cry? I wondered. *I love my grandpa, but for some reason, I just can't cry.*

Within a day or two, all the family was in town, including my uncle Richard.

He was the "rich uncle" in Phoenix who had left Denver many years earlier to make his fortune. And he had.

But he had missed the radical transformation my other uncles experienced. He had heard about the power of the gospel during countless calls from my other uncles and my ma, but he had adeptly changed the subject whenever they brought it up. He was the last Jesus holdout in my family.

Uncle Richard was the suave one, and he was, for the most part, happy with his life. He had a nice home, a beautiful wife, great kids, and a booming business. He didn't need Jesus like his brothers and sister, most of whom had hit bottom in some way due to life and strife. God had gotten Jack's attention during his multiple stints in jail. Bob had turned back to Jesus in desperation in the back seat of a squad car. Dave's scars from the battlefields of Vietnam had left him ready and willing to embrace the message of the gospel. And Ma's soul scars from a wild life were finally being salved by the forgiveness of God.

But Richard was doing just fine without Jesus in his life.

Still, the other uncles were determined to win the fight for his soul. As in the barroom brawls of old, they wouldn't stop fighting until a clear victor was declared. They were determined to knock out his unbelief, leaving it crumpled and defeated in a pool of Christ's blood.

Grandpa's hospital room and the waiting room formed the ropes of the boxing ring in which my uncles would tag-team fighting for their unsaved brother's soul. But Richard knew how to fight too. He was an expert at diverting conversations, batting away direct attacks, and locking the conversation down when necessary.

Jack took the first direct frontal approach while we were sitting in the stark, sterile, uncomfortable waiting room. "Hey, Richard," Jack asked, "you want to go to heaven to see Dad someday, right?"

"Yup," Richard said, abruptly standing to end the conversation. "Hey, I got to use the john. Where's the bathroom in this place?" Without waiting for an answer, Richard hastily retreated from the room. "I'll be back in a few," he announced to no one in particular.

After a quick pit stop, Richard decided it was safer to wait in the hallway. But Bob intercepted him there and tried a new, less aggressive approach. "Richard, I want to talk to you about something when you get a few minutes."

"Let's do that, little brother!" Richard said. "But first, let me go see Dad."

It went on that way for the next few days. Jack, Bob, and the other brothers repeatedly tried to land a gospel punch, but each time, Richard bobbed and weaved and played rope-a-dope to avoid getting knocked out by a Jesus jab.

All the while, I watched Grandpa struggling to breathe, his eyes still rolling back and twitching as my grief-stricken grandma sat by his bed day and night. It broke my heart to see my grandma so broken. But still, my eyes shed no tears.

What is wrong with me?

Every day after school Ma and I made our way over to St. Anthony's North. I would sit in the waiting room doing homework, occasionally going into Grandpa's room. I knew that Jesus could do miracles and that although the doctors said he was "brain dead," God could raise him up in an instant.

Ten days into Grandpa's hospital stay, while doing my math homework in the waiting room, I overheard four of my uncles conspiring.

"Richard said he has to head back to Phoenix for a few days to take care of his business," Bob explained. "We still haven't reached him with the gospel. We need to hatch a plan."

"Dad ain't got much more time," Jack said. "I've seen death before, and he's startin' to rattle as he exhales. That's a sign he ain't got much time."

"Agreed. He's got the death rattle for sure," Dave said, nodding. He'd seen death far too many times himself.

"What do we do about Richard?" Tommy asked, concerned about his brother's soul.

"I have an idea," Bob said conspiratorially before his voice trailed off into a whisper. I looked up from my algebra problem and leaned over, trying to hear what they were saying, but I couldn't make out any of their words.

Grandma came into the waiting room from having been with Grandpa, and they waved her over into their whispering circle.

"I agree," she said. The first glimmer of a smile I'd seen in more than a week played on her face. Then, almost in unison, they all looked my direction and started walking across the room toward me.

My heart beat faster and faster as they gathered in a semicircle in front of me, but I kept my head down and my pencil scribbling numbers. Finally, I couldn't take the suspense anymore and looked up. "What's going on?" I asked.

"Greg," Jack said, "when Grandpa dies, we want you to give the message at the funeral."

"What?" I asked. "What do you mean?"

Bob took over. "For Dad's funeral," Bob explained. "We'll get some pastor to officiate, but for the actual sermon, we want you to give it."

I was in shock. Why would they ask me to preach at Grandpa's funeral service? I was a mere teenager. Sure, I had won a preaching contest or two at Arvada Christian School, but this was no preaching competition. This was a real funeral service, and it was for someone who was the closest person I had ever had to a dad, my grandpa. This was no job for some "preacher boy." This was a job for a real preacher.

"Why me?" I asked, stunned by their request.

"Because you'll give the gospel clearer than them other preachers," Jack growled—not in anger; he just always growled.

"I heard that time Yankee let you preach in church, and you gave the gospel real clear," Bob said.

"Clear gospel" was a term that Yankee had used again and again in his sermons. He talked about some gospel presentations being clear, some being unclear, and some being false. My uncles knew the value of giving the gospel clearly, because it was a clear gospel presentation of simple faith in Christ based on his finished work on the cross that had reached all of them.

Anything that reeked of "turn or burn" turned them off and frustrated them to no end. The gospel that had saved them was one they had received by faith, not achieved by works.

"I agree," Tommy added in his calm, affirming voice.

"Me too," Dave said, giving me a nod and flashing me his big smile.

"What about Yankee?" I asked by way of encouraging them to get someone else. I wasn't so sure this was a good idea.

"Yankee's the best, but Grandpa never went to Yankee's church," Tommy said.

"What, are you chicken?" Dave asked, testing my manhood. Suddenly I felt six years old all over again, exposed for all to see my weakness and fears.

"No, I'm not chicken, I'll do it," I said, falling for the challenge almost instinctively. The last thing I wanted was for my uncles to think I was a coward when it came to one of the few things I was actually developing a talent for.

"Good!" Jack said, punching me hard in my arm—which was our family's version of a hug, a playful but solid hit to the shoulder which frequently packed enough punch to leave a bruise.

It was hard for me to take in. These were some of the same tough guys who had laughed at me when I opened my traumatic doll Christmas present a decade earlier. Now they were asking me to preach at the funeral of their beloved father.

Something was happening that I couldn't quite make sense of. For the first time in my entire life, my uncles were acknowledging something about me that I was especially good at. And that was churning some emotions inside me that I'd tried to keep tamped down for years.

I was in the process of unwrapping a new present, but this time it wasn't a doll. It was something different, something better—a gift, not from my tough Uncle Dave, but from my loving Father God.

"And there's another reason we want you to preach at Dad's funeral service," Bob said.

I braced myself.

"Richard will be there, and we all think he may be more open to hearing the gospel from a family member than some preacher he doesn't know," Bob explained. My uncles smiled at each other, knowing this was the best plan.

"What do you think, Grandma?" I asked.

"I wouldn't want anyone else to preach at Grandpa's funeral than you," she said simply, tears brimming in her eyes.

Grandma's belief in me was all I needed to hear.

Less than a week later, Grandpa died. A few days after that, Uncle Richard was back in town with his wife and kids.

The entire family—uncles, aunts, and cousins—was gathered at the funeral home where the memorial service was taking place. I was nervously pacing in a side room with the "real pastor" who would handle all the details of the service, leaving the sermon alone to me. Hundreds of people filed in quietly to pay tribute to my grandfather.

As I peered outside the curtain that separated the clergy from the crowd, I was surprised and more than a little intimidated by how many people were in the auditorium. "I can't believe how many people knew my grandpa," I said to the officiating pastor.

"Your grandpa was a well-respected man," the pastor assured me.

I was nervous. Not only were there several hundred people

filling up the pews, but my entire family was there. Plus, I wanted to do a good job for my grandpa. I wanted to honor his memory with a sermon worth hearing.

My uncles, aunts, cousins, grandma, ma, and brother lined the first several pews. Many of them were already crying even before the funeral service had officially begun. Every time one of them glanced up toward the large open casket holding my grandfather's body, a loud burst of wailing would shoot up like a blasting rocket from the Mathias-filled pews.

Uncle Richard was crying too. He, his wife, and his kids filled most of the second pew on the left. He was strategically positioned in the seat closest to the aisle—ready for a quick escape if he felt cornered.

Out of all the people in the auditorium that day, Richard was the one I was most passionate about reaching with the gospel. My other four uncles had full faith that I could reach him, and I didn't want to let them down.

"It's time," the pastor said. "Let's make our way to the stage." The pastor held back the curtain for me. I could feel every eye on me as I walked up to the stage wearing a suit that was a size too big for me—the closest size on sale in Montgomery Ward's bargain basement. It was all that my ma could afford.

The pastor walked forward and welcomed everyone and gave a quick eulogy of his own that included his fond memories of Tom Mathias Sr. A soloist sang my grandpa's favorite hymn, "In the Garden." It stirred my emotions a bit, bringing back memories of Grandpa singing it in his beautiful tenor voice at little Bethany Baptist Church. But it was not enough to make me cry.

Then it was my turn to preach. I approached the pulpit and

looked out at the crowd. In front of me, there were no longer three judges, as in a preaching competition. Instead there were five hundred judges crammed together, waiting to critique my talk. But I was preaching to reach one in particular—my uncle Richard. His response was more important to me than anyone else's in that entire crowd.

My hands grasped the sides of the pulpit and trembled. Taking a moment to scan the crowd, I silently prayed, *God, give me power to preach*.

Then I launched in. I told stories about my grandpa. I shared verses to comfort the crowd in their grief.

There was a certain authority that came from preaching God's Word. There was a certain rush that came from moving people emotionally and spiritually that I had never experienced to this degree.

This was no practice session. This was no competition. This was no showcase of a young preaching prodigy. This was me standing in God's place, preaching God's message. This was me using my best illustrations and unpacking Scripture the best I knew how in a way that the people would comprehend. This was me fighting Satan for the souls of lost men and women, and especially for the soul of my uncle Richard.

But it wasn't just me. It was God's Spirit surging through my spiritual veins, like lifeblood, giving me power to preach. I could feel his power. It both scared me and excited me. Because, even in that moment, I could tell that this kind of powerful preaching, and the biblical authority that came with it, could be easily abused. It could become the adrenaline rush that my uncles had craved right before a fight, back before Jesus changed them. It could become my idol. Instead of idolizing the adulation from having big biceps, I could easily fall into the trap of idolizing the adulation and the power that came from preaching.

God, help me, I whispered in the silent sanctuary of my soul as I continued to preach, not wanting to lose the presence of God's power due to the pride of making people cry.

Then I gave the gospel and an invitation to respond. My four years of training under Yankee served me well. Every Sunday morning, Sunday night, and Thursday night at Youth Ranch, I had heard Yankee give the gospel and give the invitation, so I gave the gospel and the invitation exactly as I'd heard it at least five hundred times before.

"Can I have everyone bow their heads and close their eyes?" I asked the crowd, many of whom were moved to tears by the message I had given.

They did.

"With your heads bowed and eyes closed, I want to ask you a question. Do you know for sure that you will go to heaven when you die, like my grandpa did?"

I could hear the sniffles and sense the conviction sweep over the crowd like a brisk breeze.

"If not, then I beg you to put your faith in Jesus right now."

Looking to my left, I was surprised to see that my uncle Richard had not bowed his head or closed his eyes. He sat there with his arms crossed and a look on his face that simply said, *You ain't gettin' me, boy!*

Looking away from Uncle Richard so he wouldn't feel like I was singling him out, I repeated my instructions. "Again, with heads bowed and eyes closed, if you've never put your faith in Jesus to save you, today is the day of salvation."

Glancing back, I could see that he still had his arms folded and was almost imperceptibly shaking his head no, his eyes wide open, glaring at me.

My uncles and aunts had their heads bowed and their hands over their faces, but they were all peeking between their fingers in a not-so-discreet way, craning to see if Richard would raise his hand and trust in Jesus when I gave the cue.

"If you're ready to put your faith in Jesus, then say this silent prayer to God in your heart right now," I continued. "'Dear God, right now I believe that Jesus died for my sins and rose from the dead. I trust in Jesus alone to forgive me for all my sins. I receive your gift of eternal life right now. In Jesus' name, amen.'"

Here was the moment we'd all been waiting for, the reason why my uncles had asked me to give the sermon. "With heads bowed and eyes closed," I repeated as a subtle reminder to the audience that the invitation was not yet done, "if that message made sense to you and you are trusting in Jesus today, for the first time, and are receiving the gift of eternal life, would you raise your hand right now?"

The invitation to respond was the test of true power in preaching—in the evangelist's textbook, anyway. Would I be able to draw in the net, to reap a harvest of souls, to see the lost converted?

Hands went up all over the place. Heads were bowed, eyes were closed, tears were shed, souls were saved.

This was gospel preaching. This was what it was all about. The thrill that ran through me at seeing so many respond to the gospel shook me to the core. The gift my heavenly Father had given me had come into full view. The last piece of wrapping paper had been removed. That Christmas gift Uncle Dave had given me all those years ago could have sent me into a tailspin of sin and rebellion. Instead, it sent me on a ten-year search for my true identity and significance and purpose, which had eventually brought me to this pulpit.

This was the gift that God had given me to give to the world. I had found my sense of security in my Father—my heavenly one. I had found my purpose behind a pulpit. God was calling me to preach the clear gospel of grace to as many as I could and to call as many Christians as I could to do the same.

But as I turned toward Uncle Richard, his eyes were still open and glaring as he shook his head no. My heart sank. But when I glanced down the row at my other uncles, I knew none of us were going to give up on reaching Uncle Richard. If today wasn't his day of salvation, we would just keep praying and sharing until that day came.

As I took my seat after the invitation and let the officiating pastor close out the memorial service, God was still doing a work in my soul. Looking at my grandpa's open casket, I couldn't help but think of how a coffin had been open and waiting for me so many times in my young life. The grim reaper had sought to take me again and again. From almost being aborted, to being close to bleeding out, to a burst appendix, through a double-whammy dog attack, to a most embarrassing near-death by butterscotch candy, I'd survived against the odds.

But God had protected me for a purpose. He'd sent rescuers (like my uncle Tommy and aunt Carol), doctors, a thought ("stand on your head"), and maybe even an angel. I was born for a purpose. I was rescued again and again *for a purpose*. And this was the purpose: to advance the good news of Jesus to as many as possible.

As I scanned to my left and looked at my uncles, all but one smiling and nodding at me, something hit me.

Like the rest of my rough, tough family, I was a fighter too—a different kind of fighter, an unlikely fighter, but a fighter nonetheless. My power was not in my biceps but in my Bible. It wasn't in my fists but in my faith. I didn't wield a gun, but I did wield the gospel.

Two weeks after the funeral, I headed toward the living room where Grandpa always sat watching television. I needed to ask him a question. It hadn't really sunk in yet that he had passed and gone to heaven.

When I turned the corner into the room and saw his empty chair, the realization hit me like a rogue wave of grief. I fell to my knees and wept for the first time since my grandfather passed.

CHAPTER 22

FLASHBACKS FROM HOSPICE

TWENTY-TWO YEARS LATER, I was sitting by Ma's hospice bed at Lutheran Hospital. Each night, when I was not on the road as an evangelist to teenagers, I slept on the unfold-into-a-bed hospital chair next to her. Day after day, I held her work-roughened hand and watched her slowly pass into the presence of the Lord. Slowly is the operative word. My family dies hard. It had been almost forty days since she first arrived, but she was still hanging on. But now she had the death rattle, the same one my grandpa had on his death bed so many years ago.

It would be soon.

I heard them coming down the hallway—the family, that is, and I mean all of them. My brother Doug, uncles, aunts, and cousins filled the waiting room, a few at a time cycling into my ma's hospice room on a steady rotation. They had just gotten back from lunch in the hospital cafeteria.

Once they had adjusted to the reality that my ma was going to die, they started recounting stories, telling jokes, and having a grand old time.

Death was nothing for us, or for my now unconscious ma, to fear. For the Mathias clan, it meant the last stop before heaven on the highway of life. Death was a mere bump in the road. The highway stretched into eternity beyond the bump.

Just a few days earlier, when my ma was still coherent and not in a stupor from the higher and higher levels of pain medications, she had me read her some of the passages from Revelation 21 and 22 over and over again:

I saw "a new heaven and a new earth," for the first heaven and the first earth had passed away, and there was no longer any sea. I saw the Holy City, the new Jerusalem, coming down out of heaven from God, prepared as a bride beautifully dressed for her husband. And I heard a loud voice from the throne saying, "Look! God's dwelling place is now among the people, and he will dwell with them. They will be his people, and God himself will be with them and be their God. 'He will wipe every tear from their eyes. There will be no more death' or mourning or crying or pain, for the old order of things has passed away."

REVELATION 21:1-4

No longer will there be any curse. The throne of God and of the Lamb will be in the city, and his servants will serve him. They will see his face, and his name will be on their foreheads. There will be no more night.

They will not need the light of a lamp or the light of the sun, for the Lord God will give them light. And they will reign for ever and ever.

REVELATION 22:3-5

These passages had brought her immense comfort.

For five weeks, whenever a new nurse came into our room, Ma would say in her raspy smoker's voice, "My son's got something to tell you." Then Ma would get a great big smile on her face as she listened to me share the gospel with them.

She wanted every one of her nurses to have the same hope that she had. Ma knew that her son was just the one to tell them about Jesus.

But now her smile was gone, and she was about to be gone too.

The nurse on watch was frazzled because my family, although saved, was really, really loud. Not only was their noise level disturbing the other patients, but my uncles had also been going into different rooms sharing the gospel with the other hospice patients.

My uncle Jack sneaked into an elderly Jewish woman's room and said, "What do you have?"

She answered weakly, "Stage 4 cancer."

He said, "That's what my sister's got two rooms down. She's goin' to heaven when she dies, because she's put her faith in Jesus. Have you?"

This lovely lady said, "I'm Jewish, son."

Jack just smiled and said, "Jesus was Jewish too. You're halfway there! Just trust in him now!"

This was normally a place for quiet recollection and

grieving, but my large family had turned this hospice into a loud family reunion. When I approached the viscerally frazzled but too-afraid-to-say-anything nurse on duty, I jokingly told her, "Ma'am, I need to warn you."

"About what?" she said, looking up from her computer, startled.

"The crazy half of my family is about to arrive," I said. I thought she was going to pass out on the spot. Of course, I was joking. The whole crazy family was there already.

Walking down to the waiting room, I could hear my family telling stories and cracking jokes. Even though the waiting room was another fifty feet down the hall, I could clearly make out every word because of their North Denver volume.

Taking my seat in the Mathias circle, I listened to my uncles tell story after story. Memory lane for my family was full of blood, bruises, and Bibles. And anything but boring.

As I silently listened to them recounting stories, there was one theme underneath them all, one scarlet thread that bound them all together: the blood of Jesus Christ. He was the final story, the ultimate hero, the one "tough enough" to redeem the "crazy brothers."

Every single one of them.

Inviting me into the storytelling, Bob looked at me and said, "Greg, tell the story about Uncle Richard, that time he came to Grace Church with all of us."

"Yeah, tell that one!" the other uncles affirmed.

I knew they weren't asking me to tell the story just for them. This story was really for the cousins who had married into the family and the kids who had been born since, who were gathered in the waiting room.

"Well," I said, "Uncle Richard had flown into town to see the whole family."

"Yeah, after he'd gotten the cancer," Jack interjected.

Before I could commandeer the story back, Bob jumped in. "It broke my heart to see him so frail. He had lost so much weight from the chemo and the cancer that I could pick him up in my arms like he was a little kid."

"We'd tried to share the gospel with him again and again over the years, and he'd just kept shutting us down," Jack explained.

"Yeah, that was until we finally got him to agree to go to Greg's church," Bob said, smiling at the memory.

It actually wasn't *Greg's* church. It was *Grace* Church.

Right out of college, my buddy Rick and I had planted a church and called it Grace Church. This was the same Rick who was my friend at Arvada Christian School. The same Rick who attended the Bill Gothard seminar with me.

We called it Grace Church because we'd finally broken free of a lot of the legalism we'd encountered growing up. Both of us had realized that God's grace isn't just good for the sinner who believes; it's good for the believer, too. We were thankful for the passion for evangelism we had encountered in our King James–only, by-the-book, hair-off-the-ears fundamentalist upbringing. But the accompanying lists of dos and don'ts and wills and won'ts had failed. After all, it wasn't evangelism we were in love with; it was Jesus. He was the reason we shared the gospel. He was the hero of our stories too.

"I thought *I* was telling this story, not you meatheads," I interjected. After an awkward pause, there was a collective roar of laughter.

"Go ahead and tell the story then!" Jack said, still laughing.

"So," I continued, "you guys finally convinced Richard to come to Grace Church so he could hear your little nephew, yours truly, preach."

"We knew you'd give the gospel," Uncle Bob interrupted.

"And we had tried again and again to tell Richard ourselves, but he shut us down every time," Uncle Tommy explained.

"It looked like our church was getting invaded by some biker gang," I said, jumping back in before they hijacked the story again. "Between the uncles, aunts, and cousins, the Mathiases filled the back two rows of the church. And, as before, Uncle Richard was sitting at the end of the pew, just as he did at Grandpa's funeral—"

"—Ready for a quick escape," Uncle Dave said, interrupting despite my best efforts.

"So, I preached the sermon and got to the gospel and the invitation as quick as I could," I continued. "All I was thinking about was giving Uncle Richard one last opportunity to believe. I asked everyone to bow their heads and close their eyes. And everyone did."

"Everyone except us," Jack interrupted again. "We were peeking through our fingers down the aisle, looking to see if Richard would raise his hand."

I picked it up from there. "Then I said, 'If that makes sense and you're trusting in Jesus and receiving the gift of eternal life through faith for the first time, then raise your hand right now.' And *boom!* Uncle Richard raised his hand, and *bam!* all you guys started bawling."

"That was one of the best moments of my life," Jack

said. "My brother was saved!" The other uncles nodded their agreement.

"At the airport later that day," Bob said, "Richard pulled me aside and said, 'Brother, before I get on this plane to go home, I want you to know something. You're gonna see me in heaven someday. Today, I trusted in Jesus.' Although I already knew because I was peeking too when he raised his hand, I just started cryin' like a baby, and we just hugged each other and cried our eyes out 'cause we knew this would be the last time we'd see each other this side of eternity."

As I looked around the hospice room at my aunts and uncles, I could see their eyes full of joyful tears. That was the day the last Mathias had fallen. All of us had been transformed by the gospel of grace.

"And in the next three months before he died," Jack added, "Richard led more people to Jesus than most Christians do in their entire lives."

"Makin' up for lost time," Dave added.

"And soon," my brother Doug said, breaking his long silence, "Ma's gonna see him again in heaven." His cheeks glistened with tears.

"Yup," I said, unable to hold back my own tears as my sweet wife, Debbie, squeezed my hand comfortingly.

"She's gonna see Mom and Dad, too!" Uncle Dave said.

Everyone nodded. We all missed Grandma and Grandpa so much. I didn't know until years later how much of a prayer warrior Grandma had been. Long before Yankee entered our lives, Grandma was desperately pleading with God for the salvation of each of my family members.

"This life we've lived," I said, rising to my feet to go check on Ma, "it's been a wild ride!"

"D— straight!" Jack said on behalf of the entire family.

As I walked back down the hallway to Ma's hospice room, my mind scrolled through the wild ride of my life. Those growing-up years were so far in the distant past but so present on my mind. From my long string of near-death experiences, to my soul-rattling personal challenges, to my family's radical transformation, to my own discovery of my calling and purpose, I was overwhelmed by God's providence.

With each step down that long hallway, I silently thanked God for the change he'd wrought in me and in my family. He had transformed them all from warriors into, well, warriors for Christ.

Warriors for Christ was the original name of the evangelism training ministry for teenagers I started soon after planting Grace Church with Rick in 1989. My uncles were all, in a very real sense, warriors for Christ. So was Ma. So was Doug. So was I.

Maybe naming the ministry Warriors for Christ was a subconscious shout-out to how the power of the gospel had transformed all of us. Maybe it was a reminder to myself that my enemy, the devil, who came to steal, kill, and destroy, was an enemy I had been, in a sense, flipping off since the third grade. It captured the intensity I felt in my heart about reaching the lost for Christ.

Thankfully, I met Debbie while attending Colorado Christian University. She was just as passionate about Jesus as I was but was polite, proper, kind, and compassionate. She helped me realize that effective evangelism is equal parts relational and relentless. I had the relentless side, and thankfully, she had the relational side. Eventually, we married. Eventually, I changed the name of our ministry from Warriors for Christ to Dare 2 Share. For me, "dare" caught the relentless side of evangelism, and "share" caught the relational side.

As I walked closer to my ma's room and approached the nurse's station, I couldn't help but notice the stressed look on the hospice nurse's face. It triggered the memories of my own stress years earlier. After planting Grace Church and launching Dare 2 Share, I was stressed too. Over a ten-year stretch, Grace had grown to over a thousand people, and Dare 2 Share weekend conferences had been picking up steam, moving from large churches to small arenas. With increased budgets came increased stress. But I was doing what God had called me to do . . . or so I thought.

Then on April 20, 1999, at 11:21 a.m., two fully armed teenagers walked into Columbine High School and viciously murdered twelve of their classmates and a teacher before turning their guns on themselves.

That day shook Denver. That day shook America. That day shook me down to my calling.

There were school shootings before Columbine and after, but somehow this massacre became the terrible yardstick by which every school shooting would be measured.

"Bound for Hell" was all I could think about when I heard what happened at Columbine High School. The news coverage that night showed hundreds upon hundreds of teenagers, after hours of hiding in their classrooms, running out of the school single file in long lines, trying to escape the madness. They had no idea whether the shooters were alive or dead.

As I watched the news footage, I couldn't help but imagine that dreaded sign on each of their foreheads. I couldn't help but think of how desperately the next generation needed Jesus to rescue them from sin's grip and Satan's clutches.

It was right after the Columbine High School shooting that I began to realize that I was no longer called to be a pastor to adults but a full-time evangelist to teenagers. I knew I wasn't an apostle, but I also knew that I had an apostolic calling to reach and mobilize the next generation. My calling was to raise up a generation to reach their generation with the power of the gospel, the same gospel that had transformed so many people back at Youth Ranch, the same gospel that had transformed me and my entire family.

Within a few months, I resigned from being a pastor and went full-time into leading Dare 2 Share. Thankfully, Rick became the preaching pastor and continued advancing the gospel at Grace Church. Thankfully, God raised up an amazing woman of God, Debbie Bresina, to lead the team at Dare 2 Share while I led the movement from the road.

As I turned into my ma's room and took my seat by her side, my eyes filled with thankful tears for all that God had done. Since the decision to resign from Grace Church and focus on Dare 2 Share full-time, hundreds of thousands of teenagers had been equipped to share their faith. A movement was growing. An army of unlikely warriors was rising up to fight for the hearts of their friends against the enemy of their souls.

Just months earlier, while Ma still had enough strength, she came to a Dare 2 Share conference in Denver. She stood in the back of the Pepsi Center and watched in pride as I shook the pulpit once again. God was using her son to rescue teenagers from the sin and shame that she had struggled with for much of her life.

Ma was proud of me, and that was enough.

As I looked at her lying there, struggling to breathe because of her advanced lung cancer, my heart was full of a strange combination of grief and gratitude.

I was grieving because I knew her time was short. I was grateful that she never knew that I knew that she'd almost aborted me. She never knew that Grandma had told me all about it at her kitchen table so many years ago. I never brought it up, because I didn't want her to know that I knew. It would only have triggered pain and shame in her already sin-scarred soul.

She also never knew that just two years earlier I had received an email from someone who asked, "Is your dad's name Toney Woods? If so, I think I'm your sister." This sister I had never met had been tipped off by Tess, Toney's sister-in-law. Tess was the only one in the whole family who not only knew about Toney's short-term tryst with my ma but also knew about my existence. Tess was the one who had told me the basic facts about my biological father when my ma took me to meet her so many years ago, a night that spun my world like the other kid had been spinning those weighted socks.

I "happened" to get that email three days before I was flying to preach in Sacramento for the first time in my life. This "happened" to be where my family, the family I never knew existed, lived.

Over email we set plans to meet for dinner. Meeting my "other family" was surreal for me and for them. Attending the dinner that night were Marilyn, my sister; Toney Jr., my brother;

a niece named Krysta; and, most awkward of all, Barbara—
Marilyn's mother. Toney Jr, like me, had a different mother as
well. My other sister, Melody, lived in Seattle at the time and
was unable to attend.

Marilyn was ten years older than me, Melody was eight years
older than me, and Toney Jr. was five years younger than me.
While everyone knew about Toney Jr.'s mom (she and Toney
had been married), nobody in the family except Tess knew
about me. Ma was "the other woman," the one in between
Toney's two marriages. But thankfully, after decades of hiding
Toney's secret, Aunt Tess accidentally spilled the beans about
me and Ma at a family reunion.

It was at that dinner that not only did I get to know my
other family, but I learned all sorts of new insights about my
father, Toney. I discovered how much of a war hero he really had
been. I discovered that, before he was in the army, he, too, was a
preacher. That's right. Preaching was in my blood. I discovered
how he lived and how he died (heart complications).

At first, when we all met in Sacramento for dinner, Toney's
wife, Barbara, didn't believe I was Toney's son. She sat in silence
as everyone else talked.

That night was full of laughter and tears, stories and
recollections, memories and magic. But all through dinner,
Barbara sat staring at me in silence.

When we all stood up to say goodbye, Barbara walked
around the table and came right up to me. She put her hands on
my shoulders, looked into my eyes, and said, "I didn't think you
were Toney's son at first. I didn't think Toney would do this to
me or to us. But now, after seeing you and hearing you, I know
you're Toney's son. I can see him in you. Toney was a hero on the

battlefield in North Korea, but he had his struggles back home. I can see glimpses of heroism in you, but in a different way. My prayer is that you are not only a hero on the battlefield of your ministry, but also a hero to your wife and kids." With that we collapsed into each other's arms in the restaurant and wept.

What a crazy, eye-opening, and emotional night that was.

Ma didn't know about that dinner meeting because I didn't want her to know. Her knowing that I had met my "other family" and was secretly keeping in contact with them would only hurt her feelings. I kept it from her because I loved her.

Taking my ma's strong hand into my own in that hospice room, my tears began to overflow their banks. My ma was about to fully realize the love that the Father had for her. Ma was about to have every last vestige of shame she ever felt stripped away in exchange for a robe of righteousness.

There, sitting next to my ma, tears streaming down my face, I was reminded that the gospel changes everything. It changed my uncles, aunts, and cousins. It changed my brother. It changed my ma.

And it changed me.

My identity was not as a fatherless kid in an earthly family; it was as an adopted child in God's. My purpose was not to fight or flex or prove my manhood; it was to mobilize a generation for Jesus. My hope was not in earning anyone's approval, even my ma's, but in basking in the love of Jesus, who gave his life for me.

In that moment, holding my ma's hands for one of the last times, I recommitted myself to the mission to mobilize a generation with that same message of redemption, hope, and love that had transformed our tribe. I wouldn't stop until every

EPILOGUE

IT'S BEEN ALMOST EIGHTEEN YEARS since Ma passed away in that hospice. I miss her so much.

Many things happened before and since her passing that did not make it onto the pages of this book. Since all but one of the chapters were written about events that took place before I turned sixteen, most of the other forty years of my life go relatively untold. Other than my brief synopsis of a few key stories in the final chapter, this book covers less than a third of my life span.

I could write a sequel to this memoir, and it would contain some crazy stories too. They would not be nearly as violent but would be every bit as interesting.

In that book I could unpack the story of an unlikely

romance between a trailer court guy and an uptown girl and how God used her, and continues to use her, to chisel off my many rough edges. Without Debbie, I don't believe I'd be writing these words to you today. As my partner in life and marriage, she has given me equal doses of confidence ("You can do this through Christ") and humility ("Don't get too impressed with yourself") that are necessary to do effective ministry over the long haul.

One full chapter of the probably-never-gonna-be-written sequel could be about my wife and me not being able to have children for ten years due to infertility issues. And then one day, a TV preacher (yes, one of *those* guys) prayed over me in a public meeting in a very uncomfortable and far-too-specific way. His prayer contained words like *sperm* and *eggs* and others that should never be spoken in a prayer meeting. He prayed them so loudly that everyone in the room could hear them clearly. My face flushed and my ears turned red from the embarrassment. But three weeks later, my wife got pregnant.

It was enough to make my noncharismatic, fundamentalist, King-James-version-only forefathers cringe.

Now my wife and I have two kids—Jeremy (age twenty) and Kailey (age seventeen—I call her "the second blessing"). Both of them love Jesus and are unashamed of the gospel. Both of them enjoy it when I recount the wild stories of my crazy upbringing and how Jesus changed everything.

One chapter could be completely devoted to the dangers of legalism. I could recount how many of the nationally known fundamentalist leaders mentioned in this book have tragically fallen in the decades that have passed since my teen years. The legalism and authoritarianism that often flow out of fundamentalism are a lethal mix that, according to Colossians 2:23, "lack[s] any value in restraining sensual indulgence."

I thank the Lord that Yankee has stayed faithful to his wonderful wife, Betty, over his six decades of marriage. I thank God that, to this day, we enjoy a strong friendship that has stood the test of time.

One chapter could be called "Friends." In it, I'd dive deeper into my lifelong friendship with Rick, with whom I coplanted and copastored Grace Church. It was the positive tension between us that created a church like no other (that I know of anyway).

I'd also tell you about my friend Art, with whom I used to regularly go sharing the gospel at local malls and parks throughout our middle school and high school years. To this day we encourage each other to faithfully and boldly share the gospel.

Then there's Zane Black. He started speaking at Dare 2 Share events over fifteen years ago. He's been my preaching partner-in-crime to reach and mobilize the next generation for Jesus and is far more relational in his approach to teens and evangelism. God has used our friendship and our unique perspectives to help make the way we train teenagers to share the gospel equal parts relational and relentless.

God has sustained me over the years through great friends like Rick, Scott, Art, Zane, Dave, Corey, Doug, Brian, Jim, Donnie, Derwin, and others. I'm firmly convinced that good, godly friends who love you deeply and speak to you honestly are a necessity for long-lasting ministry impact.

I would write about Jonathan Smith, my theology professor at Colorado Christian University and the man who helped me start Dare 2 Share thirty years ago. He showed me how to not only be a good student of the Word but also live it out with integrity, humility, and consistency.

An entire segment of the book could unpack the unique working relationship I have with my sister-in-Christ and coworker in the cause Debbie Bresina (whose name, for some reason, I pronounce as one word—"debbresina"). Over the last two and a half decades, God has used her to take Dare 2 Share from a small local ministry to a global force that is equipping millions of teenagers and youth leaders to advance the gospel worldwide.

While we were on a ministry trip in Israel with over 180 other ministry leaders, God called us to take Dare 2 Share global. Our vision statement expanded to "every teen everywhere hearing the gospel from a friend." We won't stop until all one billion teenagers on the planet have had every last chance to hear, understand, and respond to the good news of Jesus.

Just as Yankee mobilized us, a group of teenagers in Arvada, Colorado, forty-plus years ago, Dare 2 Share is collaborating with youth leaders to mobilize the current generation of teens. We do that by providing gospel-advancing resources (like the Life in 6 Words faith-sharing app and other evangelism-training curriculum) as well as catalytic events (like Lead THE Cause, a weeklong evangelism and leadership camp for teenagers, and Dare 2 Share LIVE, a teen outreach day where teenagers of an entire nation are mobilized for the gospel).

I encourage you to go to dare2share.org to find out more about these amazing resources and events and how you can mobilize Christian teenagers you know for the cause of Christ!

A sequel to my unique memoir would be great. But the

theme of both books would be the same: the gospel changes everything, and Jesus loves to use "unlikely fighters" to spread his Good News.

Have you been transformed by it yet? If not, just as I told my ma, I remind you of what Scripture says: "Today is the day of salvation."

Trust in Jesus right now. He loves you and died in your place for all your sins. Now, the risen Christ is offering you the free gift of eternal life through faith in him.

You don't have to say "Hell, yeah!" (Please don't!) But do say yes to this free gift of eternal life!

And if you already know Jesus, then I invite you to join in the fight to reach unreached souls with this life-transforming message. Your family, friends, neighbors, coworkers, and classmates need the hope that only Jesus can give them.

You may not feel qualified to reach them with the gospel and to fight for their souls, and that's perfect. Because God loves to use the unlikely to accomplish the impossible.

He's been doing that for thousands of years:

Brothers and sisters, think of what you were when you were called. Not many of you were wise by human standards; not many were influential; not many were of noble birth. But God chose the foolish things of the world to shame the wise; God chose the weak things of the world to shame the strong. God chose the lowly things of this world and the despised things—and the things that are not—to nullify the things that are, so that no one may boast before him.

I CORINTHIANS 1:26-29

ACKNOWLEDGMENTS

I AM DEEPLY GRATEFUL to all who made this book possible. I'm grateful for my amazing wife and kids, who patiently understood when I had to go away on yet another writing retreat, deep in the mountains of Colorado, to type away for days on end like a madman on a mission.

I'm also thankful for the Dare 2 Share board members, donors, and staff, especially our president, Debbie Bresina, who relentlessly prayed for and encouraged me as I sought to complete this hard-to-write book.

I'm grateful to Lee Strobel and Mark Mittelberg for introducing me to Don Gates, who has been a phenomenal literary agent. I also count it an honor that Lee Strobel wrote the foreword for my book. He is a true hero of the faith and someone I deeply respect.

Words cannot express how thankful I am for those I had to extensively interview for this book (making sure I got the stories right.) This includes my brother, Doug, the many members of my extended family, and other friends and mentors from the past.

I'm thankful for the exceptional team at Tyndale. It has been a true pleasure to work with them during this process.

And I am especially grateful for Jane Dratz. Over the last

decade and a half, she has edited most of the books I have written. Like a skilled jeweler, she has been able to chisel off the rough edges of my straight-to-the-point writing style and make it shine and shimmer in ways I never could on my own. Even after retiring from working at Dare 2 Share, Jane gladly took this book project on in spite of her bouts and battles with cancer. Her grit during the editing process, at times in between chemo treatments, showed me that she, too, is an unlikely fighter.

And last but not least, I'm grateful to Jesus. Without him, I can do nothing of eternal import.

ABOUT THE AUTHOR

GREG STIER is an unlikely candidate to lead a ministry like Dare 2 Share. This almost-aborted, inner-city kid from a high-crime area of Denver never knew his biological father. But when young Greg watched the gospel radically transform his violent, bodybuilding, crime-ridden family, he discovered that he had a heavenly Father who loved him and was calling him to spread the gospel to the next generation.

In 1991, Greg's calling led to the founding of Dare 2 Share (D2S)—a ministry dedicated to reaching teenagers for Christ. When the tragic 1999 Columbine High School shooting happened not far from D2S's office, Greg resigned from a pastorate at a local church to zero in on the urgent mission of D2S. Since then, God has used Greg and D2S to inspire and equip millions of teenagers worldwide to share the gospel with their peers. Through large-scale events, youth leader trainings, teen curriculum, books, and more, Greg has continuously worked to see every teen everywhere hear the gospel from a friend. Today, D2S holds training events called Dare 2 Share LIVE and Lead THE Cause to accomplish the ministry's mission to "Energize the Church to Mobilize Youth to Gospelize Their World."

Greg is widely known as an expert on youth ministry, teenagers, and evangelism, having written twenty books and countless articles on the subjects. He holds a degree in youth ministry as well as an honorary doctorate from Colorado Christian University. He has appeared on CNN, CBN, TBN, Focus on the Family, and several national radio programs and has been a featured speaker at Promise Keepers, Youth Specialties, Winter Jam, Lifest, and the Billy Graham Schools of Evangelism. Greg and his wife, Debbie, have two kids, Jeremy and Kailey. They enjoy hiking in the mountains of Colorado, going on trips together, watching movies, and laughing a lot.

GREG
STIER

SPEAKING REQUESTS
gregstier.org/speaking

BLOG
gregstier.org

FOLLOW